THE THIRD EYE

Solving problems through a systemic approach

Keen on learning only one skill?
Learn to solve problems systemically

SHIVALINGESHWAR NAIK

INDIA • SINGAPORE • MALAYSIA

ISBN 979-8-89026-775-7

I dedicate this book to
my Master*, *Srila Prabhupada,
whose divine words made my systems learning fun.

Contents

Preface

The name of this book is 'The Third Eye.' I arrived at this name by two means—a story and mythology.

In June 2021, during one of my events, one of the participants told me, "Mr. Naik, we are 3 partners and we run 3 companies. In our presence, everyone does their duty honestly and with full dedication. But when we aren't present, the work gets affected. Last year, we analyzed some quality issues with the help of an external agency that did a thorough analysis and reported that the quality issues had happened because of poor supervision. Engineers from the same agency helped us trace the supervisory errors and found that they happened when we weren't in the company. To improve this, the agency suggested putting cameras in key places so that we could track them and we did so. A month later, we came up with a bigger question, 'Who has the time to keep watching those cameras all day?' "

After explaining his concerns, he asked me a question, "How can we improve this situation?"

I told him, "Build systems."

He replied, "All my plants are certified and we never received any non-conformities in the audits related to systems from our customer. So, we already have systems in place."

I said, "I told you to build systems not to pile up certifications. You need another eye, the **third eye**, but it should not be in the form of a camera, it should be the system itself. Your system should be your **third eye**."

This is a misconception everywhere. Companies believe that by having certifications they will have systems. Don't be fooled, certification is just a portion of the three parts of systems (I will be discussing this in the second chapter). Like yours, certification is also someone's business. They will certify you to meet their business goals. Don't be proud of having systems just by getting certified. Check whether you really have them or not.

For the next hour, I explained what I meant by systems and how the participant should build them. In the end, I told him, "A carefully designed system is your **third eye**. Cameras won't ensure good work culture nor will certificates. People commonly refer to the tagline '*uparwaala sab dekh raha hai*.' But they also know that '*upar koi nahi hai*,' and nobody has the time to keep watching all the cameras to check what people are doing at their work table."

That is the origin of this book title, 'The Third Eye.' The **third eye** I am going to talk about in this book is 'the system.' By living a large portion of our lives as non-systemic thinkers, we have forgotten to see the systems around us and often fail to recognize them.

Our non-systemic training begins when our teacher in school says, "The hand, leg, eye, ear, nose, and head are all parts of your body."

In fact, they are not parts, they are systems. The simplest way to understand a system is through its function. Systems have defined function(s). They can never, by themselves, make mistakes unless an influencer(s) is/are involved. Parts cannot function separately. All they do is support the system for its function(s) or influence the system through its/their quality. Though the system's functions largely depend on the parts, the parts are not systems in themselves. This basic understanding is essential as we hardly make this distinction in our professional or business life.

The second reason for this book's name is rooted in mythology. Lord Shiva is known as the Lord of annihilation or the destroyer. Scriptures say that, in the end, He opens His characteristic **third eye** and burns down creation, making way for a new beginning. This book is going to do the same. It will give you the power of the **third eye**—burn down your non-systemic understanding and begin your systemic journey afresh.

In Buddhism, the **third eye** is seen as a symbol of enlightenment, which provides a perception beyond ordinary sight. That's what systems do. They provide a perception beyond the ordinary.

I promise you that after reading this book, you will never leave any problems unsolved and if you practice everything as mentioned, none of your problems will be repeated because none of them can make it past the **third eye**... the **third eye** annihilates.

Let's begin the journey of the **third eye**—the eye of enlightenment.

Introduction

My entry into this world of learning systems, design thinking and systems thinking began in 2011. While I was studying for my graduate degree, I got an opportunity to learn these things from an expert investigator and my first systems mentor, Akash Singh. He was an Indian working as an investigator in China for a private accident investigation agency. We met at an event in Bengaluru. That meeting itself was a coincidence but what happened next is written elsewhere. He taught me how investigators work, how they think, and how design thinking and systems thinking helps them arrive at events that led to problems. As a student, those complex concepts that were not part of my academic curriculum would have seemed less relevant to me. But Akash made sure that I didn't lose interest in what he was teaching. He saw something in me that I didn't.

One day Akash told me that investigators and researchers love to work in teams but only when the entire team is equally competent, otherwise they prefer to work alone. This is to protect their interest since they don't want it to be killed by others. I have always followed his suggestion before I included anyone on my team. Otherwise, I prefer to work alone and solve problems. He taught me even complex subjects in a simple way.

Some of the best techniques that Akash taught me were the cut-up technique (which I still use for every investigation and problem analysis), balancing certainty and uncertainty approaches, the importance of situational awareness (every incident or accident happens because of situational influences), the Swiss cheese model and many more. He taught me another important thing when we were sitting in a park in Dharwad. He was telling me how to conduct an investigation and how people try to hide essential information from investigators. He stated that the skill of extracting this information, even when it is not shared voluntarily, was what differentiated an investigator from an ordinary engineer. Akash said, "Shiva, in many accidents, all we get is just a piece of paper or a piece of metal or a part of a burnt body. Our task is to speak for those voiceless objects and listen to what they say. Don't ever think that only humans can speak. Even broken parts can speak but only an investigator can listen to them. He can observe what others won't see."

He was telling me all the secrets that no book could ever teach a 21-year-old boy and he made sure that I understood and I did because I believed him. I went to him with an attitude of submissiveness, the most essential quality of a student. He completed his investigation (he never told me about the task which made him come to India and that too, Dharwad. As far as I know, that was the only secret he kept from me). He left for China in February 2012 and I lost touch with him. In those days, I didn't have a smartphone nor I was using any social network. Back then, my world was like a black-and-white TV. By retaining my interest in what Akash taught me, I somehow managed to keep progressing in systems learning. When I sought to learn about modelling systems, I almost dropped the subject as it was extremely difficult.

At that time, I came in contact with ISKCON and underwent spiritual growth. I realised that what I was learning in Jay W. Forrester's and other systems thinking books and papers could be learnt from ISKCON books but in much simpler ways! Then, in 2017, I turned to the study of psychology. By that time, I was using my four-step problem-solving method and testing its relevance in various situations and problems. I reached a point where I felt there was a strong connection between systems thinking and psychology, as the word thinking is a psychological activity. With this new approach, I began revising whatever I had learned previously about systems. It was a painful and boring time for me but my Master, Srila Prabhupada's books made things interesting once again. The doctrine of simultaneous oneness and difference allowed me to simplify things based on which I developed my intrinsic systems concept.

When Krishna ate just one grain from the Akshay Patra and said, "I am full now," every sage's hunger was quenched. That story introduced me to the concept that satisfying systems satisfies everyone.

Despite commandeering Krishna's army, Duryodhana was killed in the battle whereas Arjuna had only one person with him i.e. Krishna and he was victorious. This introduced the systemic approach which is the only strategy that a businessman has to learn. Systems, not strategies, run businesses. Less is more. One is all.

These stories are timeless wisdom that we all have access to and all of us know these stories. Yet we don't know them in systemic terms. The lessons behind them can be used in various ways to suit our learning needs so that we can simplify things.

This book is different from other systems thinking books in many ways. Though systems are complex, I won't talk about the complexities here. I want to first make people think in terms of systems and then introduce them to their complexities. To teach systems thinking in simple terms, I developed an intrinsic systems concept so that we can analyze even complex systems with simple methods without damaging their integrity. I will start from the basic concepts and take you to the advanced levels, making learning an enjoyable experience.

Did the tree come first or the seed?

Questions like 'Did the tree come first or the seed? Was it the chicken or the egg? Male or female?' have put human intelligence to the test for centuries. From my school days, like many other kids, I was curious about finding answers to such subjective and unanswered questions. I don't remember when I heard these questions for the first time but all these years I never found anyone who could answer them.

Almost one and a half decades after finishing primary school, I found my area of interest i.e. solving problems systemically. As outlined earlier, I was introduced to the world of systems learning in 2011, graduated in 2014 and began my professional career in supplier management role in 2015. My systems learning was further expanded while working with suppliers who used to devise innovative ways to create problems rather than solve them. In addition, the methods that the industry used to solve problems did not prevent them from recurring. I understood that if I wanted to grow in this role, I must come up with an innovative way to solve problems. Just a year into my job, I developed a method called the four-step problem-solving framework. I have used this method from 2016 to date. Developing my approach to solving problems and testing, refining, and improving it has transformed my career. This simple but effective method has turned my focus to systems, and they, in turn, changed the way I applied the four-step framework. This became a reinforcing loop with one aspect helping the other while enhancing my learning throughout the process.

Today if someone asks me, "What came first, the tree or the seed?"

I would reply neither the tree nor the seed came first, it was the system. Whoever made this creation created a system initially. He did not create individual living entities, he created a system—a self-sustaining, self-maintaining, and self-balancing system. When certain conditions were met, that self-maintaining system created all of us. Even modern science talks about the same thing but not in a systemic manner. Scientists give a lot of complex explanations and conduct several experiments under, on and above the ground i.e. in space, but seem to miss a simple central concept. It is the system that created us and everything around us, not a particle. If such a particle existed, then it must be a system, not an ordinary particle.

If you learn to see systems everywhere, you can understand things better, solve problems in simple and fundamental ways, and teach this simple concept to others so that the world becomes a community of systems thinkers.

This book is the result of my learning for over a decade and over 6 years of work on systems and systemic concepts. I have used my unique and effective four-step framework to solve problems and investigate failures. Here I will present my learnings, studies, and the experiments I conducted to understand systems along with my research and some of the most important problems I worked on.

Before going ahead, I want to brief you on how this book is organized. I have written it as an introduction to most of the concepts I have worked on. Concepts like systems psychology, advanced risk assessment, and organizational learning have only been introduced here as each of them could easily fill twice the size of this book. Others that I have discussed in detail include systems structure, problem-solving, my four-step problem-solving framework, the Swiss cheese model, and the intrinsic systems concept, as understanding these models is key to becoming a systemic problem solver so that you can have the **third eye**, the eye of enlightenment.

I have arranged this book in a way that is easy to understand and follow.

The first chapter is about seeing systems as it is always better to start from the beginning. Systems learning begins with learning to see systems. I have presented a simple way to see and understand any system in less than 3 minutes. I have introduced the three fundamental characteristics of a system and the 6 basic considerations in building a system.

The second chapter is about understanding systems. Once you see them with your eyes, the signal gets transferred to the mind for analysis and further understanding. Here, I will draw your attention to my definition of a company and an organization so that you can use these words while considering systems. In this chapter, you will be introduced to concepts such as certifications are not systems, strategies alone cannot run your businesses and others. Systems thinking is about seeing and understanding systems everywhere and in everything.

The third chapter is about quality. You know a lot about quality already. Instead of providing publicly available knowledge, I am going to show you how quality improvement can be implemented in a company/organization and how systems can help you achieve your objectives.

The fourth chapter is about problem-solving. This is my favourite field and the centre of my daily working life. Check if the method you use to solve problems is according to the systemic approach. I have divided this aspect into two parts. In chapter 4, I have explained the four-step framework that I have used all these years along with an example on which I worked a year ago. That investigation not just solved a problem but also taught a large global company many lessons. I also introduce problem categorization based on various factors. This will help you identify systemic factors clearly and how to take care of them in your solution. This is important as leaving any factor untouched could essentially put your system at risk.

The second part of the problem-solving aspect is provided at the end of the book where I have taken the previous example and explained it using the Swiss cheese model. To the best of my knowledge, this is the first time this model is being used for operational problem-solving.

The fifth chapter is about the intrinsic system, a concept I use to make my systems analysis simple yet highly effective. Systems are complex in their entirety. Especially, the larger the breadth, the more complex they become. Hence, it is necessary to simplify them. But as a systems thinker, you should ensure that you don't break a system randomly just for the sake of simplicity.

The sixth chapter is about organizational learning. You might have heard this concept before but I have some important and new concepts to present here such as organizational learning is different from learning organizations. You will also learn how you can create a learning culture in an organization by becoming a systems thinker.

The seventh chapter is about systems psychology. You will not find this word anywhere. Through my work in systems and systemic ways of solving problems, I have understood that to improve them, you need to focus not only on the systemic approach but also on the psychology of your systems.

Going through the sequence is very important as the system is all about practice. Every chapter creates the level of understanding needed for the next one. So I recommend reading the chapters in the given order so as to not miss any essential concepts. These will help you become a systems thinker and a systemic problem solver. Reading and learning is also a system, so follow it.

Remember: Every non-systemic solution incurs a debt to the system's way of solving problems, and the systems know how to get us to repay it. For instance, climate change is classic proof of this truth. Solving problems systemically and thinking in systems respects the systems that run our lives, our businesses, our world, and everything we ever know and will know. Without systems, there is nothing. Help them help you in turn.

Chapter 1

Seeing Systems

First things first, systems thinking involves the ability to see the whole. The systems view of the world means to look at the world in its simplicity, not its complexity.

The first law of ecology says, "Everything is connected to everything else."

This is the fundamental idea of systems thinking. In any system or systemic environment, everything is connected through certain relationships. In simple terms, understanding these relationships and simplifying them for solving problems is what systems thinking is all about.

This book is about systems thinking, organizational learning, and systems psychology. Don't worry if you are very new to these words or have never heard them before. I have made it very easy for you to understand.

For four years, I used to teach systems in their whole form to my suppliers. Two years ago, while investigating a field failure, I realised that systems are highly complex in their entirety and I began studying them to simplify their understanding. In the meantime, I received a challenge from my mentor.

He said, "Shiva, explain systems understanding in no more than three minutes."

That challenge was hard but I accepted and started working on it. By that time, I was working on the intrinsic systems concept and the role of psychology in systems understanding. I conducted a series of experiments at my vendors' sites and studied books, journals, research articles, and a lot more. Finally, after three months, I arrived at a way to teach systems in just three minutes. That was when I understood the real pain of simplifying complex concepts. It is very easy to make a subject complex. Take a big topic, study its basics, and try to explain it to others. This is the reason why the world is full of people who make things more complex than they are. But, remember, our analytical mind is very lazy and people always want to stay away from complex things that demand mental effort. Despite the subject's importance, they choose to stay away because of its complexity and the corresponding effort needed. That is what that behavioural scientist understood and he wanted to teach me that by asking me to simplify it.

I found my eureka moment when I scrolled through my mobile to delete some photos. I told myself, "This is the easiest way to explain the intrinsic systems concept."

I have represented it in the photographs below. Study them and make a note of your observations before turning the page to read.

Figure 1.1

Figure 1.2

Both photographs are of The Great Banyan Tree taken in 2018 during my visit to Acharya Jagadish Chandra Bose Indian Botanic Garden, Howrah, near Kolkata, India.

The first picture was taken from a distance in which the tree is captured in its entirety, whereas in the second, you can see the areas within the tree i.e. individual prop roots. That's all! If you have understood this, you are halfway through your journey to seeing systems, understanding intrinsic systems and becoming a systems thinker.

A board displayed near the tree notes, "The Great Banyan Tree is more than 250 years old and spreads over an area of about 1.6 hectares with about 3618 prop roots. A wonder in the plant kingdom, it occupies a position in the Guinness Book of World Records."

Why is it a wonder in the plant kingdom? This great tree was damaged by two cyclones in 1864 and 1867 when some of its main branches were broken. This exposed it to a severe fungal attack. Its main trunk decayed and was removed in 1925, but still, it grows vigorously. The characteristic of this banyan tree is that aerial roots grow on the branches and run vertically toward the ground, and they become prop roots for this wonder of the plant kingdom.

The Great Banyan Tree is a great example for understanding the concept of intrinsic systems. Just like the prop roots of the tree, every system has self-sustaining roots based on which the system operates. Perfectly structured systems—intrinsic systems—operate the entire system even though some functions are not performing as they have to be or at least help you see the real problems.

Now, let me cite another example to bring more clarity as understanding this concept is crucial to getting the most out of the other concepts in my work.

All of you know McDonald's. You may have visited McDonald's restaurants—a perfect place for your taste buds. Do you think you'll find the same menu or taste in their New York and Delhi outlets? Will you find the same culture in their Tokyo and Durban restaurants? Why is there a difference? If you look more deeply, even with those differences, McDonald's maintains its standards. Why is that so and how is it possible?

In every country across the world where it has its outlets, McDonald's serves items that represent the taste of that country in alignment with the local tradition and culture. If McDonald's standardized its menu and made the same things available across the world, it wouldn't be that much of a success. In the United States, slaughtering of cows is allowed and people like to eat beef. So McDonald's serves burgers with beef patties in the US. In India, the country and people do not like to see beef on their plates, so they serve McAloo Tikki which is familiar to Indians as most parts of the country serve snacks with *aloo* (potato). In fact, if you are from Maharashtra or ever visited it, you might even see the traditional version of McAloo Tikki, called Vada Paav. This is an excellent example of an intrinsic system. McDonald's, as a complete organization, is a bigger system (organization-centred system). In every country, it has developed intrinsic systems that work in a self-sustaining way, similar yet different.

I learned this concept from Chaitanya Mahaprabhu's preaching of the doctrine of simultaneous oneness and difference, *achintya-bheda-and-abheda-tattva*. I will go into a little bit of philosophy to clarify the concept. In Sanskrit, achintya means 'inconceivable', bheda translates to 'difference,' and abheda translates to 'non-difference.' According to India's religious movements, Hinduism has two conflicting philosophies regarding the relationship between living beings and God. The Advaita philosophy of Shankaracharya asserts that the individual's soul and God are one and the same, whereas the Dvaita philosophy of Madhvacharya propagates the dualistic argument that the individual's soul and God are eternally separate. When both these philosophies were argued widely, Lord Chaitanya taught the philosophy of achintya-bheda-abheda which includes elements of both viewpoints. The living soul is intrinsically linked with the Supreme Lord and yet is not the same as God—the exact nature of this relationship being inconceivable to the human mind.

Srila Prabhupada writes, "The soul is considered to be part and parcel of the Supreme Lord. Same in quality but not in quantity. God having all opulence in fullness, the spirit soul, however, having only a partial expression of His divine opulence."

God in this context is compared to a fire and the souls as sparks coming off the flame. This is how systems and intrinsic systems operate, simultaneous oneness and difference. The McDonald's Delhi restaurant has the same systemic standards as Chicago or Illinois but it is different with respect to the local menu, culture, and taste. This is similar to the great banyan tree, every prop root out of the 3000+ that is seen has an individual existence and also helps create a beautiful system that we call the 'wonder in the plant kingdom.' This wonder comes when we build our systems in such a way that they function with oneness and difference simultaneously.

In both examples, the central standard or system is also self-sustaining (though the main tree got damaged it didn't poison the entire tree) and so is each part. Developing intrinsic systems in this way helps us to understand the system's entirety better and aids in solving problems. We will see how to develop intrinsic systems throughout this book.

Difference between a system and an intrinsic system

Intrinsic systems are the sub-systems of the entire system. The intrinsic system influences the integrity or the quality of your main system, whether it's an organization or a product. If I look at my body as a whole system, my hands, legs, head, ears, nose, eyes, etc. can influence my body. Hence, they are intrinsic systems and not parts. The difference between a system and a part is that systems have function(s), whereas parts don't have any function. They can support or influence the system's functions. Here, your hands, legs, and ears have a function. The quality or integrity of the intrinsic system directly affects the system. On the other hand, the quality of the individual parts influences the quality of the intrinsic system. For instance, hands and legs have bones, muscles, nerves, etc. If a bone is fractured or nerves are damaged, it affects the intrinsic system and the whole system.

Identifying intrinsic systems and strengthening them strengthens the main system as well. If we analyze the entire system as a whole, it makes the task very difficult. We may miss considering one or the other factors which may lead to errors. This is especially true if you are a global organization or have a large number of product categories or are working with complex processes. This issue is common even in a small company. Using the intrinsic system concept helps in strengthening your system's defences (we will learn more about these defences when we discuss the Swiss cheese model).

Organization Centred System	Product Centred System
Management	Tool, Die, Machine
Accounts & Finance	Production Process
Manufacturing	Handling
Maintenance	Work-in-Progress (WIP) Storage
Quality	Inspection
Purchase	Packaging
Human Resources (HR)	Finished Goods (FG) Handling
Marketing	Finished Goods (FG) Storage
Customer Services	Shipping

Table 1.1

In the table above, I have detailed two verticals—organization- and product-centred systems. Looking at systems with this distinction in mind clarifies what we are looking at and the objectives that we need to derive that particular systemic environment. Whenever you observe systems being discussed in this book, try to ascertain which of the two kinds of verticals I am referring to. Both are important for solving problems and you need to understand both as problems can occur in either of these models. If you face any difficulty in understanding this distinction, more clarity is available in chapter 4 and the Swiss cheese model at the end of this book.

Systems always follow a loop

I will provide you with an acid test to check whether the solution you have developed is a systemic one or not. Write down all the influencers on a piece of paper and try to connect them. If they form a reversible loop, then what you have developed is a system, otherwise, it is non-systemic. This is why in system modelling, we study causal loop diagrams and then use them extensively to solve problems.

Take the example I used in the introduction, 'Did the tree come first or the seed?' I repeat that it is neither, the system came first. Without a fostering system, no tree or seed can survive. By looking at the food chain, you may think that the tree came first but how did it come without a seed? That is something only a system can tell you. The system has three fundamental characteristics.

To understand this better, let us go to the food chain.

Figure 1.3

There are two influencers in a food chain—the prey and the predator. You can see that the chain or systemic cycle is initiated by the flora and then moves on to the one who lives by eating it (deer) and the next link involves the earlier one becoming prey for the next member in the chain who is the predator (lion). To keep this chain in a reversible cycle, the trees developed seeds and animals developed eggs or babies. This is the system model. You will find answers to your unanswered questions when you fit them into this model.

The next common question that arises is, "Who came first, male or female?"

This is a debatable subject and divulging the details here will divert the scope of this book. So to move ahead, let us consider that the system brought both in at the same time!

Let us look at another example and then go on to learn what the systems can teach us. In the water cycle seen below, it is difficult to state where it begins and where it ends.

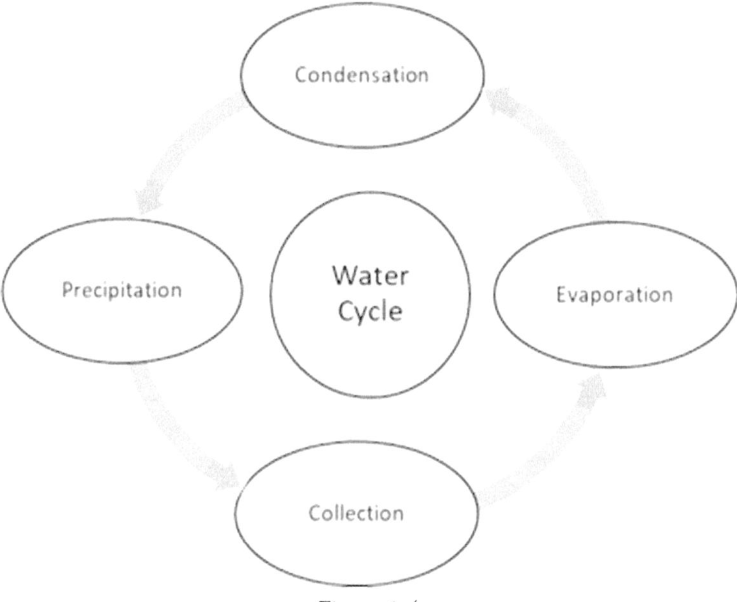

Figure 1.4

It runs cyclically and if we look at the system behind it which keeps it running, we can see that the different seasons help this cycle. There are different climatic conditions to balance the system and a lot of activities happen in the systemic environment by themselves. Everywhere, the system does all the work according to its designated objectives and considerations.

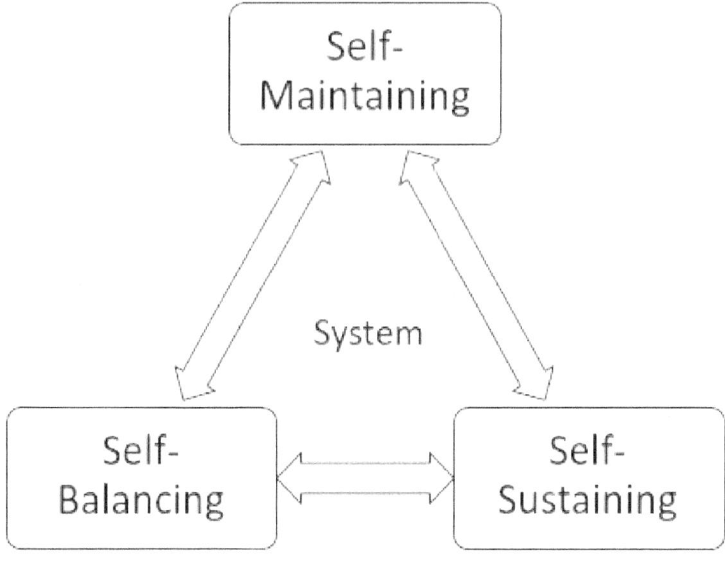

Figure 1.5

The natural working of any system is designed with three fundamental characteristics. The three fundamental characteristics include self-maintaining, self-sustaining, and self-balancing. Look at the food chain and water cycle again and observe how systematically they are designed. The trees are limited by grazing animals and the number of animals are limited by their predators and the predators are limited by the system itself.

As you move from left to right, you will see that the number of predators reduces to make sure that enough food is available to sustain that entity—trees are more in number than deer, which are more than the lions. This is the self-sustaining characteristic of the system. Despite having a higher life expectancy, some animals like humans lose their reproductive ability to maintain the system's self-balancing ability. A well-designed system maintains these characteristics unless there is an attempt to alter it through external intervention to create disturbance in the system structure. For example, poaching animals, damaging the climate and ignoring its defences.

An important point to note is that any well-designed system has a self-maintaining ability, i.e. it emits signs or signals whenever an influencer tries to disturb the system artificially. This alerts us to take the necessary corrective measures to reinstate that system to its prior mode and function. If we ignore those signals then one day we will have to face the consequences i.e. the system may stall as every system knows how to defend itself.

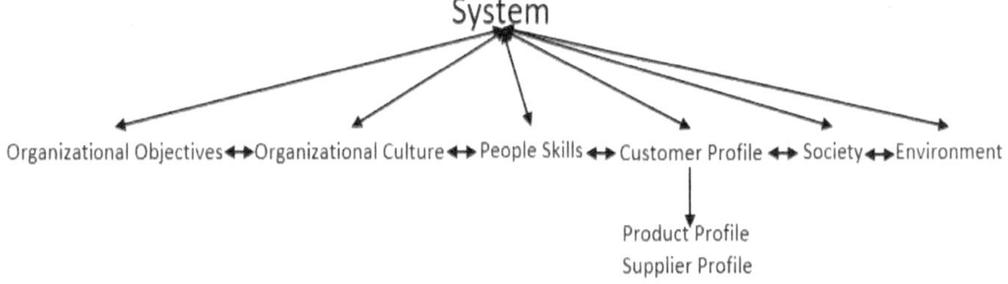

Figure 1.6

The six basic considerations[1] that are taken into account while designing a system include organizational objectives, organizational culture, people skills, customer profile (including product and supplier profile), society, and environment. Every member in these 6 considerations influences the others in both ways (forward and backward) (see Figure 1.6). Every great system structure is designed by considering all these parameters so that it can achieve its three fundamental characteristics.

- **Organizational objectives:** These may include a mission statement, vision statement, values, quality policy, sustainability policy, and so on. The objectives are the reasons why your organization exists. You may define it in terms of either financial or societal goals. Some people say that emphasizing financial objectives can project an image that you are more focused on money and this may give the wrong message to your customers and employees, but this is

1 Note: After this section, I will mainly focus on the organizational context and I have defined the six basic considerations in those terms too.

not true. A good financial position is necessary for the organization but you should not run your company just to earn money. You should create a purpose for its existence and make an impact, something that can happen only when you have an excellent objective. Everything starts with a clear, concise, and well-structured objective.

- **Organizational culture:** The type of leadership, hierarchy, communication channels, and the type of behavioural culture your organization fosters, etc.
- **People skills:** The skills of your employees should be aligned with your organizational objectives, culture, product profile, and customers. Irrespective of their skills, you must have skill upgradation as a part of your growth plan. Education is the one-point solution for every problem. Organizations have no formal existence, it depends on the competency of the people working for them.
- **Customer profile:** This also considers product and supplier profiles. To ensure that your customers are satisfied, both your product and supplier profiles should be in proper alignment. Customers thus become both the centre and perimeter of your business as considering the customer profile in designing systems brings clarity to the function. You don't need to design separate systems for individual customers, however, we will discuss this in detail in the chapter on understanding systems.
- **Society:** Every system should consider social objectives too. Gone are those days when business was all about self. Now every organization must have social aspects included in their business continuity plans. We will discuss this topic again in the chapter on organizational learning where I will talk about the holistic sustainability model.
- **Environment:** Environment can stand for two things—nature and the market. Your sustainability policy must talk about nature and as an organization, it is your responsibility to protect nature and natural resources. At the same time, an organization should also look at market movements, like competitors, new entrants, technological innovations that may disrupt the old ways of business, and any other factors that may pose a threat to its growth and existence.

In some systems standards, we may learn these 6 considerations in bits and pieces under the context of organization and stakeholders management but the problem with learning them piecemeal is that we miss the inter and intrarelationships between them. In designing systems structure, this relationship component is a defining factor.

Basics and fundamentals are not the same. Basics are related to the structure whereas fundamentals are related to the characteristics or principles.

Chapter 2

Understanding Systems

Systems are all about their structure. You don't need to be highly qualified to become a systems thinker. Though it is a very special skill, it can be learned and practised by anyone by following a few simple steps.

The systemic approach is the simplest way of solving the most complex problems. The principle of this approach involves being simple, learning in simple ways, and working for simplicity while solving complexities. Since systems do all the work, positively influencing them has to be your number one priority so that they can achieve their fundamental characteristics.

Every organization has evolved over time to reach its current status. Its life cycle begins with a business, grows to a company, then to an organization, and finally into a global organization. To understand this evolution in detail and the concepts involved in the process, some of the key terminologies you should be aware of include:

- **A business:** When an entrepreneur starts his/her entrepreneurial journey, he/she establishes a business individually or along with a set of partners, hires friends and a small group of relatives. At this point, the objective is to survive i.e. to ensure that the business won't crash. You can say that it is a start-up. Normally businesses during their start-up days work without formal systems or work with non-generalized practices (the owners themselves work as a system).
- **A company:** As the business grows, it passes the survival stage and its products or services become available in the market. Now, the entrepreneur(s) has to hire people to cater to the market demands. The business has become a company. It has a team, an objective, etc. The difference between a group and a team is that for a group, there is no objective or common goal. The group may work on its own, and initially, it is necessary to know which idea works. Survival is the only purpose at this stage and the group works towards developing products or services that fit the market.

  But, when the business becomes a company, it has a team. It has passed that painful survival stage and understood what fits in the market. Now it needs to align its products or services to the larger market needs. For that, it needs to have an objective and a common purpose, not an individual way of working.

  The entrepreneur continues to act like a father, fostering a system that is not very deep or broad since it is still working locally and is mainly handled directly by people. Often such companies work in semi-systemic ways. They follow the systems sometimes or bypass them at other times. The management strongly believes that systemic importance is limited to some functions alone, like quality. It's similar to following a basic version of the formally structured system.

- **An organization:** The company grows further, expanding its market, establishing product lines, and improving quality consistently. Now the company cannot work only with one team. Having only a common purpose doesn't work anymore, it needs a system. A system helps you achieve both efficiency and effectiveness to develop excellent products and ensure consistency in the process both in terms of quality and quantity. There can be no compromise as you have to fulfil the market demand with quality products. Only a system can help you in achieving this broader objective. A company truly becomes an organization when it establishes a strong system and implements it across all functions. This results in the team working within the system and across its length and breadth while solving problems.

The defining criterium for a company growing into an organization is not financial but systemic strength. You may reach a billion dollars in financial statements but if you don't have any systems or don't work with a strong systems approach and if your people don't work as a team, all you have is a business. It is neither an organization nor a company, it is just a business or a struggling start-up.

Whenever I use the word organization in this book, it refers to a company or business working with systemic depth and breadth, solving problems systemically, and educating people from the system and for the system. These terminologies are very important to obtain maximum benefit from my work. Another difference with respect to an organization will be detailed later as it needs to be understood at a much deeper level.

Most of the experiments and examples I outline subsequently are from the manufacturing industry, more specifically from the auto industry. However, they can be applied across industries—be it a restaurant or an airline. Since systems are everywhere, the concepts are the same. I repeat—we are systems, we live in a system, and the organization where we work is also a system. We live in and around systems so this book is not only for the manufacturing industry, it is for everyone. Whether you are an employee or an employer you have takeaways here that can substantially change the way you work and the way you solve problems and at a broader level, the way you look at the world.

If you want to improve your system, then focus your efforts on its structure. In 2019, I did an experiment called 'Cognitive Vibrations' to analyze the effect of systems structure on the company's performance. There were 21 participants from various functions in one of my learning sessions at my supplier's premises. They were facing repeated complaints from almost all the customers. I analyzed the situation and soon understood their concerns. They had recently been certified for an International Automotive Task Force (IATF) certification without making an effort to analyze systems structure and its alignment to the company, customise it and review the suitability of the documents to the company's culture and the skill level of its people. I didn't want to give them training on how to prepare standard operating procedures (SOPs), structure documentation, etc. I wanted to show them how to learn systems and their operation in the real world. I chose 5 participants from each of the quality and manufacturing functions and asked them to take 4 videos of operations and analyze those videos at different times. For example, during office hours, after dinner, just before going to bed, at midnight if possible, immediately after getting out of bed, etc. I asked them to even show them to their kids and note what they said.

The next day they handed their notes to me. There was an astonishing revelation! Our brain processes the same information differently at different times. The influencers in this information processing have a key role, influencers such as the people around us, the environment, conditions, situations, and importantly, the kids.

One participant noted that personal protective equipment (PPE) wasn't mentioned on the SOP while he was riding a bike. Another participant, who jumped a signal and paid a fine, understood the importance of observation and following standard practices. Yet another participant's kid helped him keep track of the spelling errors on the documents as some of them changed the entire meaning of the sentence. This is how every great idea takes shape. If you are doubtful or want to understand something in depth, use the benefits of your cognitive vibration. On the other hand, if you want to understand something in breadth, use the benefits of the collective cognitive vibration of your team or your family or your mentor.

I often use this technique to solve problems and have found solutions to some of the complex problems just after waking up or at midnight while studying the same pictures and data that I had scoured during the day. I use these cognitive vibrations because many times we are primed to see what we are thinking and that momentary thinking influences our thoughts. To avoid this priming effect, we need to analyze the same information at different times. I recommend taking around 3 days for general problems and at least a week for tough problems. But ensure that you keep observing your thoughts while doing different activities. These could include reading, watching movies, walking in the garden, playing with kids, painting, or writing day notes just before going to bed. All of them help tap into your cognitive vibrations and can generate amazing ideas to solve problems, by doing so you can avoid the priming effect.

Brainstorming is a popular technique professionals use to solve problems as a team. To put this in scientific terms, it taps into cognitive vibrations. But there is a problem with the way professionals use this wonderful method. Generally, they form a cross-functional team, assemble in a meeting room, and spontaneously share ideas. They discuss the problem and identify some potential causes. They then instruct an engineer to test and validate the causes so that they can establish a cause-and-effect relationship. As soon as the team comes out of the meeting, except for that engineer, nobody thinks of the problem.

This is not the way to exert your brain. The human brain is such a device that the more you exert it, the more effective it becomes. It is similar to sharpening the saw (the seventh habit). The right way to conduct brainstorming is to push the problem deep into your thoughts and process it at different times of your day while doing different activities. That's why I don't call the process brainstorming in my research. Instead, I called it cognitive vibrations.

Some people may think, "If we keep processing work-related thoughts all the time, where is the work-life balance?"

You need to remember that I am not requesting you to sit at a table, open your laptop, and do something. I am just asking you to process your thoughts. It will hardly take a few seconds, and those few seconds could save you hours or days of work in those meetings. If you learn to tap into the benefits of cognitive vibrations and exert your brain in the right way, you can maintain a better work-life balance.

Make problem solving a part of your daily life and not just a responsibility in your job description. This is about being effective to become efficient.

Certifications are not systems

It's time to redefine the system. In the next section, you will see a very simple one-word definition of a system. But as of now, we need to understand another one—a system is a set of things interconnected to achieve a specific objective called a system's function.

The above definition is made up of three parts, 'set of things,' 'interconnection(s),' and 'objective.'

- **Set of things:** This includes the 6 basic considerations detailed in the previous chapter—organizational objective(s), organizational culture, the skill level of the people, customer profile (including product and supplier profiles), society, and environment.
- **Interconnection(s):** These help in achieving the system's three fundamental characteristics. Without interconnectedness, you cannot create any system that can achieve self-maintaining, self-sustaining, and self-balancing abilities. Right from our body to this world, everything is organized in an interconnected manner. Our life is made up of interrelationships (relationships with others) and intrarelationships (relationships with ourselves). In the language of spirituality, it is called our relationship with the Supreme God. You may not believe in God but you cannot lack belief in this relationship. It is present as your system's characteristic.
- **Objective:** It is the system's function(s). Every system is created to achieve certain functions and objectives. If there are no functions, then there's no need for a system. When you develop a system to run your company, that becomes its function.

One of the easiest ways to build a system is by following certain standards. National or international bodies have identified and defined certain best practices and designed them as frameworks or boundaries within which you need to structure your organizational system. The structure is all about understanding its essence. A great system is one whose structure is designed for company-specific basic considerations.

In the preface, I mentioned an instance where a participant had told me about his company being certified. However, his people still made errors. This was because certifications alone cannot protect you. The truth is very clear, your employees are making errors because your system allows them to do so. You need to put an effective system in place.

At around 3 years of age, my nephew learned to scold others. We used to laugh at his stuttering words at that time but it became a problem as he grew up. I told my sister that kids are like mirrors. We see our culture in them. If we find our kids scolding others or using bad words, don't try to change them, ask members of the family to speak good words around them. You can really see your face and your behaviour in your kids.

The same applies to companies as well. We see our company culture, our systems, and the behaviour of our systems in our employees. Your company behaves as your system allows your employees to behave. If you receive any complaints from your customers, do not try to find out who did what, rather work on identifying why he did that, what influenced him to make that error, and what was the situation in the system at the time. Behind every error, there are influences that have led the system to compromise its objective. At a subconscious level, we are all very honest and truthful. That's the reason why polygraph or lie detector tests are accepted legally in many countries. No normal human wants to commit mistakes unless they are unaware of the consequences of their activities.

Some years ago, I was involved in analyzing an industrial accident. We were a team of 8 investigators. The task before us was analyzing an accident that resulted in two employees losing their hands! We were shocked when we saw both victims. Their forearms were completely detached, it was scary. It took us 14 days to complete the investigation and at last, what we found was a great lesson to every business. I will explain it briefly. Six months ago, the company had purchased a brand new advanced electronically controlled machine, but unfortunately, it had a faulty controller. The programme had a glitch that allowed one rapid hydraulic ram closure every 500th hour.

During our initial analysis, we didn't find anything specific. So we turned to the manufacturer of the machine and the electronics company who had manufactured the controller and asked them to share the details. They analyzed the card from the controller, tested it and reported that there was one line in the program that allowed the controller to reset itself every 500 hours. We asked them to share further details as this issue could lead to a legal case. They shared a long technical story about this happening at exactly the 500th hour. Our next question was why hadn't this happened during the 6 months since the machine was procured. We obtained an answer for that from the other operators working in the company. Actually, the double closures had happened twice in the last 2 months, but fortunately, both these incidents were during the day shift. The operators had somehow escaped and they had not reported these instances to the plant management! Digging even further into the incident, we came to know that the 500th-hour closure happens only when the machine runs continuously. If there is a power failure for more than 5 hours, the controller gets reset as the backup battery gets drained. In addition to that, three months ago, the company had purchased a diesel generator and started running the machine non-stop as the owners had received multiple new orders, leading to the initial cases of this incident.

The point here is that the operators who lost their hands were not at all at fault but they became victims. When there is an industrial accident, operators usually get blamed and it is tagged as human error. But if you really study accidents and complaints, you'll always find that somewhere the system was compromised which allowed errors to occur, just like the double closure every 500th hour! We were surprised to detect this cause but after going through the 72-page technical document shared by the company and digging into the series of events happening at the backend, we had to believe that the system had been compromised.

How and why do systems get compromised?

Systems get compromised because of our blind beliefs. We get our plants certified without putting in efforts to customize the system and align it to the 6 basic considerations. We also never study whether the system is properly interconnected to the company or not. What we believe is by getting a system certification we have a competent system in place. This is similar to the company discussed above which felt that by having the electronic controller, both operational effectiveness as well as safety will improve. But, in reality, the controller caused a serious accident.

We can understand this through a system diagram given below.

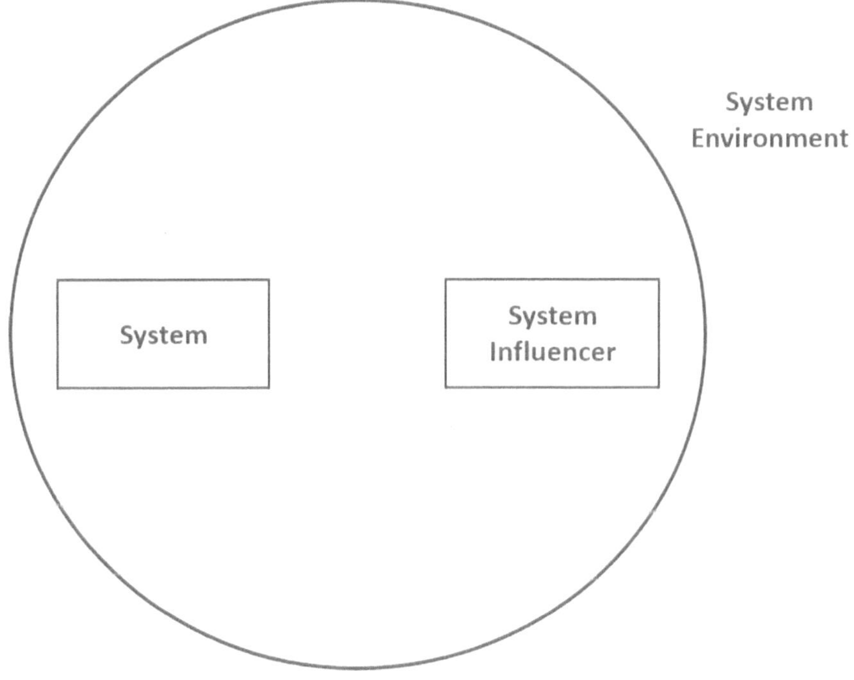

Figure 2.1

Every system has three parts:

- The system itself
- System influencer: influencers internal to the system
- System environment: influencers external to the system

By procuring certifications, you are putting only a portion (not completely) of the first part of the systemic approach into place. There is no impact on the other two parts which essentially drive the system on a day-to-day basis.

If you have a license or the skill to drive an auto rickshaw, you cannot drive a Mercedes Benz, though they are similar at a systemic level. But as the environment changes, the influence points also change. You need to know what and where the controls are. In the second case, i.e. system influencers, you need to work on identifying influence points and skills required to operate the system.

The earlier example of my nephew learning to scold was the effect of his environment and family conditions. Let me provide a professional example. If you are working in a company (where there is no system or only a semi-system), you must be familiar with managers who keep changing their opinions or directives from time to time. What they said last week may change today and what they say today will definitely change during the next week or so. Why does this happen? Why do people change their opinions and directives? This is chiefly because of the changing situation. Our situations create conditions that shape our activities or behaviours.

For example, last week, your company may have received a quality complaint. So your boss immediately said, "Quality first." This week he may have received an email from the supply chain manager that the customer line is getting affected due to short supply, so the boss responded, "Running the show is important."

As the situations change, our behaviours change too and most of the time such situations depend on external factors that are away from the direct influencers. The same applies to system functions. Based on the external influencers (the people who don't directly influence your system daily), the external environment (the company's dynamic environment like top management actions or customers' dynamic requirements), the system changes and so do the results. Though these are already considered while designing your system structure, you cannot consider the dynamic nature of these influencers and cannot deny them either. So these things need to be considered when you analyze any problems in the system or when you want to improve and enhance your system. This can be better explained by a case study of a problem that I investigated a year ago (chapter four).

Defining a system

I defined systems as interconnections earlier but now I am going to simplify it further. Let's recall how our mathematics teacher taught us to solve mathematical equations. We first write down an equation (sometimes multiple equations), fill data in the variables, and go on simplifying it till we reach a solution. This 'simplifying' is an essential skill for any problem solver. To become an excellent problem solver means to become a fundamentalist i.e. to go back to our childhood and recall how we used to learn things then. There is no need to look at things in a complex manner.

From three words, I am going to simplify the definition of a system further, to just one word. In the rest of this book, I'm going to work with that one word to show you how it will give you an insight into the **third eye**. That one word is 'confidence.'

System means confidence

In 2015, I started my professional career in supplier management. In just 6 months, I got frustrated by the practices the industry follows and from then onwards, I only worked on understanding the underlying problem(s). I realised that there was a lack of systemic understanding and the entire industry believed that system meant certification. I kicked this belief out of my mind. From 2016 onwards I started my research in simplifying systems understanding and its implementation. Along the way, I worked with dozens of clients in building systems and helping them solve problems with the systemic approach. My earlier work experience provided me with an exclusive opportunity and access to hundreds of suppliers to learn their practices and test my findings. My experience of over 7 years helped me put the definition of systems into just one word, the simplest of all the definitions, system means confidence. Yes, CONFIDENCE.

Wherever there is a system, there has to be confidence so that we can be sure of its performance. The stronger my system is, the higher my confidence will be. Investors invest in companies they are confident about. My body is my system and I do regular health check-ups just to feel confident. Your customers audit your company just to make sure you follow the requirements outlined by them, that audit gives them confidence that the products or services you are providing are consistent in quality. I visit my suppliers to assure my company that the products are safe and my assurance provides my company management with confidence.

We follow or implement several systemic practices like statistical process controls, measurement system analysis, 6 Sigma and many others to improve predictability so that we can take timely actions if there are any variations. This gives us confidence in our process. Predictability further enhances our confidence. Take any system, if it is perfectly designed and put in place, it is for one central purpose alone i.e. to give confidence.

Your customers buy your products or services because they have confidence in their quality. You fly with reputed airlines because by flying with their services you feel confident. All those backend operations of providing great quality products and excellent flying experience are done by the system.

If you look through the system's eyes, you would know that in organizations all the work is done by the systems and people only influence the working system. Work is not done by the people but by the system. A pilot does not fly an aeroplane but influences the aeroplane as an internal influencer. The aeroplane is the system here and it is designed to fly in the sky. All we do is influence the system and the system does all the work. We can make systems error-free, which means that even if the influencer wants to direct the system to erroneous results the system won't allow for it. We will learn more about this in the Swiss cheese model given at the end of this book.

Systems and alignment

Alignment helps us assess confidence, in this case, in the system. In financial or systems audits, we verify practices being followed and their alignment with the requirements. Misalignment is a sign of a problem and may cause a loss of confidence. In standard language, we call this non-systemic behaviour and non-conformance.

Verifying alignment in a systemic approach is easier said than done. Some companies do not follow standard practices while running their systems. As systems thinkers, we cannot say that what they are practising is not a system. It is one if it is working for them and aids in maintaining the confidence of everyone involved. If you observe the three characteristics of self-maintaining, self-sustaining and self-balancing, then it is a system.

A well-designed system has a self-healing capacity. It knows how to maintain its existence, and it knows how to make the process as well as the result error-free. It amazes me when companies talk about foolproofing their process. A well-known Japanese word Poka-Yoke is famously used when foolproofing is discussed. These people don't know the fundamental characteristics of a system. Your system has this capacity in its structure itself, all you need to do is design a system considering all 6 things stated earlier. If you do this correctly, you don't need a separate endeavour to foolproof your processes.

Auditors also face instances where they are unable to understand the systems and hence reject the audit. In my career, I faced some suppliers whom I rejected in audits but they used to ask me, "Sir, do my parts have any issues? Do I have a poor rating in the past? If not, then why should I invest money in systems?" This is the scenario and if you are an auditor and practice regularly, I am sure you also might have been faced with such questions.

That was when I realised that some people or businesses follow non-generalized systems, which are not aligned with the defined standard frameworks. As people who establish systems, we need to see the broader picture. Systems cannot be defined in a single framework. They are highly customizable and can be modified according to one's company structure, people skills, working conditions or say work culture, product profile, economic constraints, and the customers they serve. That is why even international bodies like ISO recommend that auditors be aware of the process that they are going to audit.

An acid test is to check two things in the current practice—is it helping you feel confident and predict the associated risks? If your answer to both aspects is yes, then you have a system. Hence, you cannot reject it but you can guide the company to move on to the next level, to build and align its system to meet the standard frameworks.

No system is a good system by default. The words 'by default' mean by chance or by luck. A good system is always the result of desired and deliberate effort.

Some of the key takeaways from this section are:

- The three characteristics of the system are self-maintaining, self-sustaining, and self-balancing
- A well-designed system knows how to maintain itself and how to sustain its existence
- The two acid tests to use whenever you come across a difficult situation like poor system demonstration but excellent performance record, check if it helps your confidence and predicts risks. If both are true, there is a system in place

I derived some more clarity from my research work on systems psychology. In my studies, I worked to reveal some of the underlying factors that govern the systems built by small companies that function extremely well for them but are not scalable. Why is this the case? The reasons are since the companies are small they cannot afford costly systems implementation and again, because they are small, many issues are sorted by direct intervention from the owner(s) who can manage things. In many cases, this intervention is very much necessary. As explained earlier in this chapter, when a business is initiated, the owners themselves work as a system, as working without a system is not possible. Moreover, without systems, reversible work is not possible, and loop or reversibility is the fundamental characteristic of a system. If you have any cyclical function or reversible loop, you have a system, though it may not fit into the standard frameworks.

Let us now move to how non-generalized systems are built. Humans have unique learning capabilities and sometimes it is very difficult to generalize them. I call such learning connections psychological pathways (or cognitive maps). The owners of companies with their experience on the job, their business, and product categories build non-generalized pathways deep in their minds through continuous evolution of trial-and-error. These pathways work only for them. If you want to run their non-generalized system, you cannot run that business even for a day even if you are highly intelligent and are experienced at running a global organization. This is because what they have built is a non-generalized system that works only for them. This may not be good but is enough for an entrepreneur to build the foundation for the business, otherwise, it may not survive. At the same time, when you want to achieve growth, you have to build a system and come out of these psychological pathways so that the professionals you hire can successfully manage your organization.

Many of my suppliers were in this category. They were running their business successfully on their own. They used to fail in every audit, but their performance had no spots. Technically I did not have any reasons to tell them why they should go for internationally validated standard systems. However, after analyzing my psychological pathways and differentiating generalized and non-generalized systems, I could support my recommendation. As customers and auditors, we should have in-depth knowledge about the systems and recognize them so that we can help companies improve their practices and jointly improve our confidence.

To explain this idea better, I will take a very easy example. When babies speak their first words nobody but their mothers can understand them, because they have built a unique type of connection that no science can explain. I have named such connections as psychological pathways. If you want to understand what the baby is saying, then its mother has to decipher the words. Their initial words are non-generalized, the world cannot understand them, only their mother can. Similarly, the owners also have built unique connections that others cannot understand unless we look through the systemic eye, the **third eye**. But, like the baby, owners should also learn to upgrade and improve their language or the systems to achieve the next level, so that not just them but others too can understand them. A business cannot grow with non-generalized systems in place.

To put this in scientific terms, let me talk about classical conditioning. Based on your experiences or trial-and-error methods a pairing of stimulus and response gets built into your understanding. Since such a pairing is based on your personal experience, those lessons work only for you. Unless you come out of this personal (non-generalized) stimulus-response pairing you cannot achieve stimulus generalization which is possible only when you build generalized systems.

Customer-focused systems

Some companies practice customer-focused systems i.e. they develop some specific practices for specific customers and customize their offerings to better serve that particular customer. This happens mainly due to a lack of systems understanding at the level of the company and the customer.

By setting up systems you can automatically serve all the customers. Do not try to satisfy everyone individually as this creates a burden on your system and it increases the risk of error as your people have to switch from one system to another to satisfy these demands. This switching between customer-specific systems affects employees. I have explained this in chapter six under the attention residue effect by Sophie Leroy. From a systemic view, this is ridiculous and people who do not understand systems can think that multiple systems need to be implemented in the same company. A well-run organization does not need multiple systemic models. When the 6 considerations are taken into account while building the system, it will satisfy every customer automatically and individual endeavours are not needed.

I have learned this from my Master at ISKCON. Here is a verse from Srimad Bhagavatam that explains the concept "by satisfying systems you can satisfy everyone" very succinctly.

यथा तरोर्मूलनिषेचनेन
तृप्यन्ति तत्स्कन्धभुजोपशाखाः
प्राणोपहाराच्च यथेन्द्रियाणां
तथैव सर्वार्हणमच्युतेज्या

–Srimad Bhagavatam 4.31.14

As pouring water on the root of a tree energizes the trunk, branches, twigs and everything else, and as supplying food to the stomach enlivens the senses and limbs of the body, simply worshipping the Supreme through devotional service automatically satisfies the demigods, who are part of the Supreme.

Another story that supports this premise is from the Mahabharata. When the Pandavas were in exile they were gifted the Akshay Patra, an inexhaustible vessel, by the Sun God. Unlimited food could be drawn from the vessel but once Draupadi finished her meal the vessel ceased producing food. One day Duryodhana planned to send Durvasa Muni along with his disciples to the Pandavas for lunch. He planned to make the Muni curse them. By the time the sage and his disciples arrived, Draupadi had finished her meal and had nothing left to serve her guests. Draupadi prayed to Krishna for help. He came and asked for the vessel. He found one grain of rice and one small piece of vegetable in the vessel. He ate the two small pieces and His hunger was satiated.

When Krishna said, "I'm full," all the sages felt satiated and they left.

The first instance is what we all can see every day. We don't water every leaf and branch of a tree. We pour water into the roots and it automatically reaches every part of that tree. The second story refers to the fact that satisfying God—the designer of this self-maintaining, self-sustaining, and self-balancing system—satisfies everyone. Both stories support a similar premise—satisfying the system satisfies all, with no need for separate efforts to satisfy individual members. The customers are also a member of your system as customer profile is one of the 6 considerations in systems design.

I will briefly explain the emergence of the multiple system concept so that you can easily grasp it. Two system auditors approach the auditees with their checklists, one with 20 points and another with 100 points. In the more elaborate checklist, auditors describe every point in detail whereas in the shorter one, they consolidate their requirements. As the auditee demonstrates the practices, the auditor will ask for more in-depth information. This does not mean that your company is wrong or you need to align your practices with their customized checklist. The auditors are just assessing the alignment of your practices with their systemic requirements. If something is unclear, then read the description or ask the auditor to describe their requirement. If you have a real system, then you have everything. It is just a matter of understanding different terminologies. For example, water in English is known by different names in other languages, such as *paani* in Hindi and *neeru* in Kannada, etc. These are just different terminologies or names for the same thing. Ensure that you understand the requirements as they may be in a different language or terminology and demonstrate your practices accordingly.

In my learning influencer programme, I have a concept called One Organization One System (actually it is One Organization One Voice) which helps bring systems culture into every company and transforms them into organizations. The purpose is very simple. There has to be only one system for a company or an organization, the multiple-system model can be dangerous as it can confuse people and lead to more errors. I have collected data from over 120 companies to study how these customer-focused systems negatively affect the company and how errors have increased in such an environment.

The key takeaway here is to satisfy the system, not the people. Companies that don't understand systems go for the customization of systems or multi-system business models. Support the One Organization One System campaign.

System is rigid as well as resilient

A good system has both properties—it is rigid as well as resilient. Though there are various other ways to understand this, for first-time systems students it's easier to understand these system properties through an example of a statistical tool called control charts. I have given a typical control chart in the diagram below.

Figure 2.2

The control chart graphically plots your process data and helps you analyze process variation. We evaluate control charts using 8 rules called the Nelson Rules. Out of these, only one rule talks about rigidity i.e. the first rule which states that all points must be within 3σ limits. All the other rules talk about flexibility, more precisely, the resilience of the system or the process (here I call the process a system, an intrinsic system according to the product-centred system). This statistical tool is used in analyzing problems and building predictability within the system. If you know how to analyze the control chart, you can detect the problem by looking at the trend of the line. You can also assess what the process could lead to in the future.

Along with the control chart, the intrinsic system concept also helps in analyzing rigidity and resilience. Take our earlier example of McDonald's restaurants. Every restaurant has to function strictly under corporate terms and conditions. There is rigidity. But at the same time, these restaurants have the freedom to choose their menu and adjust the taste as per the local needs. This refers to resilience. Take any good systemic examples, rigidity and resilience are in-built, again not by default, always as a result of desired effort.

In design thinking, I teach the 3C concept. These are competent, compliant, and constraint. I use this 3C concept for design reviews before I approve drawings that can be shared with my suppliers. As a designer or a design thinker, you should ensure that your designs and drawings are competent enough to be manufactured [designed for manufacturing (DFM) and designed for six sigma (DFSS)], and are compliant with the customer's requirements. In order to make them competent, you cannot jump over the customer's requirements, you have to be compliant. Thirdly there should be no constraints.

The first law of improvement says, "Anything you cannot measure you cannot improve."

So, measurement is necessary for improvements. Many designers define excessive constraints in the name of achieving better compliance with requirements. These unnecessary definitions of constraints don't help. As a design reviewer and design thinker, it's your task to ensure that the design is free from unnecessary or poor constraints. In engineering, we use Geometrical Dimensioning and Tolerancing (GD&T) to define constraints. GD&T provides the design with resilience but an accomplished designer will know the technical concept behind it to create the right balance between resilience and rigidity. Remember the 3C concept and understand it to become a better design thinker—competent (yes), compliant (yes), and constraints (no).

Design thinking: Balancing assumptions and imagination

Every designer knows the importance of assumptions and the scientific role they play in designing something. In any engineering design, designers make a lot of assumptions like the expected load to carry or the suitable physical shape. While designing your car, the designers don't know how you drive the car. They just make assumptions and get the car tested through various laboratory and early field tests.

Assumptions are also a kind of imagination but the former are scientifically valid and experimentally proven, whereas the latter can involve wild guessing. Still, to become a design thinker, you should know how to imagine things, hence the right balance of these skills distinguishes a designer thinker from a designer.

I will not go into what role psychology plays in imagination and how some of the great design thinkers learned this rare skill of imagining. Instead, I will quote an instance from the book 'Leading Apple with Steve Jobs' by Jay Elliot. The author talks about one of his interactions with Steve Jobs. I always refer to this example when I talk about design thinking. When the team of iPod developers showed an early model to Steve Jobs and said, that they had used an absolutely minimum case size for the device, Steve took the device and dropped it in the fish tank. As the device sank, he saw air bubbles streaming to the surface.

He gestured to it and said, "See? There's still space left, remove it."

Jay writes, "The team went back and made the iPod smaller."

Steve asked the designers, "Why should my customers pay for the space?"

This is a design thinker's thought process. Steve didn't run the model through hi-tech software. He used his imagination or his common sense and dropped the device into the water to assess the availability of space.[2]

2 Note: This specific example is more than common sense. It is the rare skill of imagination that some people have mastered through imaginative learning. But to explain that concept, I will have to take you through a complete set of psychological factors which is not within the scope of this book. Hence, in this case, it can be denoted as common sense.

Strategy and system

No strategy can create magic unless you have a fostering system in place. First, we will learn what this strategy is all about and then we will understand how the system is the best strategy of all.

One key definition for strategy comes from Bruce Henderson, the founder of BCG, a top strategy consulting firm, "Strategy is a deliberate search for a plan of action that will develop a business's competitive advantage and compound it."

You will find different types of strategies in business books. For every activity, there are dozens of strategies such as production strategy, marketing strategy, sourcing strategy or strategic sourcing, costing strategy, quality strategy, financial strategy, leadership strategy, managerial strategy, and whatnot. I visited a business park in Bengaluru recently for some work. In the security room, I was surprised to read a strange poster which was entitled 'Security Strategy!' There were 19 points listed below it for the security personnel to follow and this was called 'Strategic security management.'

I remember thinking, "Wow, I think this was the only area that was not covered. That's done too."

If you keep reading books on strategy, there will be no end in sight as each author will write what he/she knows or has found through his/her comparative analysis. For example, books like 'Good to Great' or 'Blue Ocean Strategy' have been written by authors whom I respect. They have done a fantastic job but I strongly feel that Good to Great would have been even better if the author had followed a systemic approach and presented lessons in terms of systems, instead of a comparative study. The book compares one company to another in the same industry or product line. The one that earned more money was deemed successful.

Steve Jobs said, "Being the richest man in the cemetery doesn't matter to me." Money should not be the criteria for measuring a successful human being or organization.

The pitfalls of comparative analysis can be explained by a story from the Brihadarnyaka Upanishad. It is the parable of the blind men and an elephant. A group of blind men heard that an elephant had come to their town, but none of them had felt its form and shape. One day, they decided to go and touch it to learn its shape. With the help of another person, they approached the elephant. The first blind man, whose hand landed on the trunk, sensed a thick snake. For another, whose hand touched its ear, it seemed like a fan. Another person, whose hand was on its leg, felt that it was like a tree trunk. The fourth one placed his hand upon its side and said that the elephant was like a wall. The fifth blind man who felt its tail described it as a rope. The last person felt its tusk and stated that the elephant was hard and smooth, like a spear.

The moral of the parable is that it's not about who is right or who is wrong but what the fundamentals are. Psychological research has proven that we may be blind due to lack of eyesight and also due to our limited capacity to understand and interpret things. We may thus live in an illusory world. We compare other things to what we know and try to justify our understanding without looking at the bigger picture and maintaining a holistic approach.

You can come up with a new strategy every day like an eating strategy, sleeping strategy, walking strategy, reading strategy, and exercising strategy. The list is endless.

The bigger question is where is the big picture view in this? It's like getting trapped in the reductionist world and talking about the big picture view which is not possible. In fact, I also loved strategy when I was preparing for my MBA, but once I understood that systems give bulletproof solutions I dropped the plan and moved to systems. I have worked on and even given sessions on Supplier Partnership Strategy but decided to drop it later and moved to systems completely.

In 2021, as a part of my systems psychology research, my mentor asked me to attend an online event about 100 strategies. I came to know later that more than 9000 participants had attended that event, and I bet, most of them are still confused about which one would really help their business. He wanted to teach me how a large number of choices affect our decision-making ability.

Before going into the details of this subject, I would like to segue into an experiment that I conducted to study the effect of a large number of choices on the decision ability of humans. My team and I conducted this experiment in 2021, almost 3 months after I attended the event about 100 strategies.

How does our mind work when we are offered more choices?

While working on the curriculum for One Organization One System Campaign under the learning influencer program and systems psychology, I wanted to know how a large number of choices affect our temptations and how our ability to decide is affected by multiple choices. Though I had collected some data informally via conversations and interviews with my colleagues, I wanted to conduct a formal experiment to analyze it in detail.

The purpose of this experiment was to understand how the human mind works when it is offered more choices. The title was Chocolate Choice experiment and the plan was as follows,

- First stage, children of 7 to 8 years were offered 100 chocolates
- Second stage, adults of 40 to 45 years were offered 100 chocolates
- Third stage, the children from the earlier group were offered only 2 chocolates
- Fourth stage, the adults from the prior group were offered only 2 chocolates

The entire experiment was conducted with 40 participants. The results in males and females were recorded separately.

I bought 100 different chocolates, about half of which were imported from France, the UK, the USA, Japan, and South Africa. The choices contained both vegetarian and non-vegetarian chocolates to cover a wider range of tastes and choices. As mentioned above, 40 children were selected for the experiment. The chocolates were arranged in a perfectly designed layout on a table and the children were allowed to choose the one they loved. Each child was allowed to choose only one and the selected chocolates will be refilled immediately to ensure their availability for other participants.

This first stage of the experiment took 6 minutes to complete. Only 4 kids selected their chocolate in under one minute. A notable observation and learning from the experiment was that 14 children, about 35% of the total, did not select any chocolates and said, "Mummy *daategi,*" i.e. My mom will scold me, or "Chocolates *khane se daton mein cavities hoti hai,*" i.e. eating chocolates can cause dental cavities, etc.

In the second stage, we tried the experiment with 40 adults, 30 of them were from a business background and 10 were professionals, all aged between 40 and 45. A similar set of 100 chocolates was arranged on a wider table with a slightly different layout. Here, I expected that the adults wouldn't mention their mom at all, because of their age. But, about 16 of them i.e. 40% of them avoided the chocolates since they led to diabetes or because their doctor had told them to maintain a sugarless diet, etc. We accepted this as most people in their forties do become more health-conscious. That was my reason for choosing this age group.

A separate and interesting part of this experiment began when I asked my team to give 2 chocolates randomly to the same participants, but not as a part of the formal experiment. While giving them, I asked my team to repeat the excuses they had used earlier for not taking the chocolates. However, when we reached out separately with 2 chocolates, every kid and every adult accepted them! Their replies to our comments were,

- How would my mom know if I have eaten chocolates at school or the playground?
- Two chocolates won't create dental cavities
- Yes, the doctor told me to maintain a sugarless diet, but it is okay if I eat one or two chocolates less frequently

This is how our ability to choose gets affected when we are offered multiple choices. In the first stage of the experiment, both the kids and adults thought that we were asking them to eat all, even when the instructions were very clear that they needed to pick only one.

When we did the same experiment with girls, they also made similar comments but in a lesser proportion (only 4% of girls and just 10% of women). It took girls significantly less time than boys to pick their choices. Girls finished in 4 minutes and women finished in 5 and a half minutes!

The lesson here is clear: more choices greatly affect your ability to choose. A 100 strategies won't benefit you. On the other hand, they will keep you away from everything and you will start thinking, "Is strategy so difficult to learn?"

You might feel overwhelmed by the choices in front of you and may not be sure about which one to choose. This is somewhat similar to your response when you go shopping in a large mall. You either buy nothing or buy everything or more than what is necessary. I hope you understand that both are negative effects!

This experiment clarifies one truth: More is more dangerous than less

My father used to often tell me that in their time it was very difficult to get information so people remained unaware of the facts. In contrast, we now have everything at our fingertips and still, people seem unaware of things. Earlier it was non-availability but now it is the excessive availability of information. Both are causing the same effect—unawareness. We need to learn how to consume information.

After scouring through hundreds of eBooks, our students get settled on Facebook. A husband and wife sitting in the same house share photos on Instagram, talk through YouTube videos and spend time on Amazon Prime. If you think having access to more information, more resources, and more amenities is good, you are wrong! It affects you negatively. If you want to understand what I mean, observe your mental responses whenever you walk by or scroll through choices.

This is the reason why even after becoming an engineer my mathematics is much weaker than my father who never finished his 3rd standard. He had no access to calculators so he learned it all by pencil and paper when he started his provision stores in his 40s. Engineers are trained to use calculators. They aren't trained in mathematics but in using calculators. This is why passing high school in the 1970s is considered tougher than getting a master's degree in the 2020s. This is also the reason why our parents hardly use Google to recall the Prime Minister of India when the country applied LPG to revive its economy. I bet that you just googled what LPG means, it is liberalization, privatization, and globalization. That's how information available at our fingertips made us blind (psychologically blind).

Even after drinking Horlicks and Complan, our children use more Google than our parents who still ask, "*Yeh harlick kya hai?*" i.e. What is this harlick? They are unable to even pronounce Horlicks, let alone taste it. Having more information is not good.

More is more dangerous than less. Learning all the strategies in the world is more dangerous for your business than not knowing its definition. Still, if you would like to use the word strategy in your playbook, then learn only systems strategy—how to build and improve systems.

Comparing strategy and systems

Though I never teach my clients strategies, sometimes they do ask me to provide them with some strategy to improve their systems. I advise them to use any strategies they like to develop and strengthen their systems. I caution them, that strategies alone cannot run their business or company or organization unless they have strong systems in place. Wherever there is/are process(es), a system exists, irrespective of whether you believe or identify its presence. If you do, you can strengthen it and use it in your favour, otherwise, you will become a victim of systems failure.

I studied the bankruptcy patterns of businesses over the last 50 years. I found that most of them if not all had powerful leaders. They were well educated, experienced with a qualified team, had enough resources, good pay packages, and above all, they were largely aware of various strategies. Yet their companies sank to the bottom of the ocean like Edward Smith helped the Titanic settle on the Atlantic floor. The reason was that they did not have systems in place. They failed to see how their companies were trapped in non-systemic behaviours. As you will recall, every non-systemic solution incurs a debt and the system knows how to get it back from us. Even if you had a system when you started your business or company, you have to work on strengthening it continuously as and when you see problems. Identifying and solving them systemically can help it achieve its three fundamental characteristics. If you don't work on it continuously, it will be similar to owning an iPhone that is not updated. Bugs in the system will crash your phone.

Check global history—great governments, great organizations, great empires—anything that was great, became great because they understood how important a system is for them and worked hard to build one. That was the secret of their success.

Do you know why McDonald's or Apple or Facebook or any great organizations in the world became global?

They cleared the clutter early in their journey, which made them see clearly what matters to their business and what really customers care for. Many businessmen think that by having a long list of product offerings they can get more sales, but sorry to say this, it is not so. It makes you struggle to keep up with the rest or worse, it takes you out of the business faster. When the McDonald brothers revamped their hamburger store, they had only 3 products, yes, only 3—burgers, finger chips (French fries), and milkshakes.

Ray Kroc writes in his masterpiece, 'Grinding it Out,' "The simplicity of the procedure allowed McDonald's to concentrate on quality in every step, and that was the trick." Less is more.

	Consumer	Pro
Desktop		
Portable		

Figure 2.3

When Steve Jobs returned to Apple, his priority was to prevent it from going bankrupt and restore it as per his dream. In line with this, the first thing he did was draw a 2x2 matrix. He placed only 4 products on the list and asked the team to delete all others. He cleared the clutter, and the rest you know, is technological history. The picture above shows the 2x2 matrix that Steve presented at the 1998 MacWorld presentation. It is simple and free from clutter. Less is more.

Carmine Gallo in his book 'The Innovation Secrets of Steve Jobs' writes, "Steve Jobs had cut Apple's total product offerings from 350 to 10, a significant reduction by anyone's standards. Simplifying Apple's product line ultimately helped resuscitate the company, leading to one of the most successful financial decades of any company in U.S. business history. By simplifying everything—product offerings to product design—Apple leapfrogged its competition, creating easy-to-use products that stunned reviewers and brought joy to millions of customers around the world."

Facebook wasn't the world's first social network platform. The failure of earlier social networks gave its founder Mark Zuckerberg an important warning. He was initially not in a hurry to get users registered. In fact, he received hundreds of letters and emails from university students asking for registration on Facebook.

In 'The Facebook Effect,' author David Kirkpatrick writes, "Mark was very much aware of what he was going to build and he had perfect clarity on how to reach there, 'clear the clutter.' "

Success comes one step at a time. Do not get trapped in the clutter of choices. Build systems instead of menu cards or long lists of products or services. If you conduct an in-depth study of McDonald's, Apple, Facebook, Salesforce, Oracle, Amazon, Alibaba, Tata, Reliance, or any great organization, you'll see why they became successful. The founders never saw their creation as a business. All they did was design a system that achieved the three characteristics that I have mentioned above—self-maintaining, self-sustaining, and self-balancing.

Even my master, Srila Prabhupada, instructed his disciples, "All the temples must be self-funded. There should be no fund transfers from one temple to the other."

This is the way of building a system. Building a system means arranging 6 basic considerations in a loop that achieves three fundamental characteristics of a system. Master did not build any temples, he built a system and even after 45 years of his physical absence, the system is working and will work in the future as well since it is self-sustaining. That is a real system.

The system is like an eye into your business. You cannot imagine the real existence of your business without having a system. When your business is smaller, you need a smaller and less capable system. It may not be immediately observable, but in reality, you have a system, you act as a system and help your business function properly. When you grow that business into a company, you should also grow your system, you cannot do everything.

Another test is, to check for a holistic view as strategies do not offer holistic solutions. If they did, you will not need a different strategy for each aspect of your business. On the other hand, every system is complete in itself. It is holistic and reversible and it knows how to manage itself and balance its existence. Whenever I teach systems, I do not teach different models for security companies and directors. It is not needed. To design any system, all you need are the 6 basic considerations. Since company cultures, objectives, and people skills vary among companies, their combinations never match. So no two systems are ever identical. That difference in systems itself is a competitive advantage. Hence, you need not worry about competitive strategy.

Figure 2.4

The renowned author of the book 'Competitive Strategy' Michael Porter talks about the five forces analysis. In my initial days, I used the book often and even today I refer to it sometimes. This works because it is a systemic approach. But he has taken only 2 of the 6 considerations, customer profile (suppliers and buyers), and environmental considerations (external environment). He has taken only 2 because he was a strategist. Like a reductionist, he has broken things into multiple non-related ways and given piecemeal solutions. The reductionists offer solutions in bits and pieces as they view individual parts and lose the forest view, which is the basis of a systemic approach. Missing even one consideration may lead to systemic problems.

As systems thinkers put it, "A system is more than the sum of its parts."

There is a two-way relationship between the systems parts and their influencers. Unless you consider all 6 considerations and identify their relationships (inter and intra) and study the influences, you cannot build a strong and reversible system with the three fundamental characteristics.

If you have systems, you don't need strategies, and if you don't have systems no strategy can save you. It's very clear. Every failure in history, from empires to organizations, tells the same truth.

Don't sell products, sell confidence

Imagine that you are a customer. What do you want to buy? What do you care for? You don't mind what strategies I use to produce products and provide services. My use of strategies and technologies has nothing to do with you. As a customer, you are only interested in the quality of the product you are buying and the confidence I am selling you. By this time you already know that the confidence comes from the system. Both quality and confidence are the products of systems. Good systems produce great products, and great products establish great confidence. Work on building great systems. Business is always simple, don't make it complex and get stuck in the labyrinth of your misadventures.

Coincidently, on the day I completed this section, I received my copy of the Special Edition of Harvard Business Review (Spring 2023 edition). It was entitled, 'How to Think More Strategically.' I quickly went through the contents and one section on page 86 drew my attention, 'Stress Test Your Strategy: The 7 Questions to Ask.' I have briefly listed those seven questions below. First, think like a strategist and write your answers to the questions. Second, after reading this book, write your answers once again, but in systemic terms. Then compare both of them and you'll see how simple it is to think about those seven questions with a systemic approach. Whichever business book you pick in the market, each one talks about the same 6 basic considerations. Every business or company or organization aims to achieve three fundamental characteristics. Why should you take a round trip when you have the easiest and safest approach to reaching your destiny?

The seven questions are:

1. Who is your primary customer?
2. How do your core values prioritize shareholders, employees, and customers?

3. What critical performance variables are you tracking?
4. What strategic boundaries have you set?
5. How are you generating creative tension?
6. How committed are your employees to helping each other?
7. What strategic uncertainties keep you awake at night?

Every word in that spring 2023 edition can be simplified through a systemic approach.

Marketing: System or strategy?

In my systems career, whenever I say, "Business is not about strategy, it is about systems," I have always faced this question from the owners and marketing professionals, "Mr. Naik, we agree that systems are necessary for solving quality-related problems, but I don't think they will help us in marketing our products. For that, we must have marketing strategies. Are there any ways to use systems in marketing?"

I usually reply with another question, "Tell me what you want to achieve through marketing. Are you trying to impress your customers or trying to influence them?"

If you are trying to impress customers, it means that you are attracting one of their senses, not all of them. Put any of your marketing strategies in this five-sense model of marketing and you'll learn an amazing lesson. In this information-rich age, people have no interest or time to see your ads. That's the reason we get ad-free subscriptions to YouTube, Amazon Music, and Spotify because people don't want to see ads. We don't want to be impressed. On the other hand, if you try to influence people, nobody can deny the impact. For example, Amul's ad campaigns, Apple's Think Different ad campaign, etc. People still go to YouTube and search for Apple's ad campaigns. They talk about more than their products, they influence people to buy products and take part in impacting the world.

Give your customers a reason to come to you. Not opportunities, reasons. This 'give a reason to come to you' is what I call a systemic approach to marketing. If you build a great system, you develop and manufacture and make excellent products available, your customer service will be amazing because you have systems. All these aspects influence your customers and give them a reason to come back. We repurchase some products even before we need them just because we have a reason to do so. Those products influenced us so much that we cannot afford to lose them.

We may think, "What if they run out of stock by the time I need them next week? Let me go now and buy them."

Here, the manufacturer or service provider is giving them a reason, not just an opportunity to come and buy their product. If you go to any supermarket today, you'll find over a dozen options for every product. They all are opportunities but only excellent products produced out of great systems give the customer a reason to buy, and hence we buy them.

If you want to market your products or services, try to influence the customer's mind and all the senses will follow automatically. This is one of the things psychometric marketing teaches us. Even if you can run a successful marketing campaign, if you don't have a system at the backend that can produce excellent products and amazing services, you'll not be able to convert those leads into sales. Have you heard the famous marketing cautionary line 'Great branding of bad products kills your brand faster?' The systemic approach prevents you from falling into this trap. When you combine psychometric marketing with systems psychology, the view becomes crystal clear.

Chapter 3

Quality

When it comes to improvement, quality is a psychology

What is quality? The ASQ or American Society for Quality defines quality as 'the characteristics of a product or service that bear on its ability to satisfy stated or implied needs' and 'a product or service free of deficiencies.' In essence, the definition of quality is fit to perform or fit for use. This is its theoretical definition.

Joseph Juran, one of the quality pioneers, developed a 3-step quality management tool called the Juran Trilogy—quality planning, quality control, and quality improvement. So, how can you improve quality? According to Juran's managerial process, these may be the three necessary steps to manage quality but how do you improve it?

After years of working with my suppliers, I understood one reality, quality improvement is linked to psychology. If you want to improve your company's quality then improve your people's psychology. The word psychology generally makes people think of a state of disorder or a state of resistance. Their quick response is that they don't have any psychological issues in their company and the employees are cooperating well with the company initiatives.

Actually, that is not what psychology is about. The study of mental disorders is called psychiatry. Psychology refers to the study of behaviour. Psychiatrists are doctors, whereas psychologists are not. Generally, they don't prescribe medications. Psychologists are behavioural scientists and therapists who cure your disease by talking to you and understanding your unspoken and often unknown problems. Most of the time people hardly know they have psychological problems. Even if they do know, they cannot explain what they are feeling. We call such problems unspoken problems and the only way to understand them and cure them is through studying behaviours.

How your people behave in the workplace has a direct link to the quality of your products or services. By behaviour, I mean how they work, how they walk, how they talk, and how they think, all of this is directly linked to the quality of the work you have assigned to them. I did a lot of work on this since behaviour is key for quality improvement. Then how can we control behaviour? It was a question my clients used to often ask me.

Some companies have even broader and deeper problems and state, "Mr. Naik, we work mainly with temporary workers hired on a contractual basis. By the time we understand their behaviour, they will be elsewhere. It won't work. Tell me, what can we do? How can we improve our quality?"

These comments and questions motivated me to work on systems psychology. I tried to evaluate how the behaviour of the systems can be understood by understanding the behaviour of the influencers so that we can predict it and incorporate necessary controls. This will be explained in detail in chapter 7.

Let your Human Resources (HR) department supply you with new faces every day, even then you can maintain high quality. Blaming HR for a lack of people skills is an industrial habit these days. People in the manufacturing and quality sector, especially, keep blaming HR whenever they get complaints from customers. One famous dialogue states that '....this problem is because of new manpower'. Assess any low-performing action plan and you'll consistently find comments such as new manpower, lack of training, etc.

In most of the investigations that I conducted, I used to go through their previous records just to know how they solved problems. What I always found was head hiring or warm body hiring and blaming HR. I used to strongly condemn this.

However, I do accept that no matter how strong your people-hiring practices are, you cannot become an ideal employer nor can anyone become an ideal employee. Mr. Perfect is like a perpetual motion machine, PMM. This is something we study in thermodynamics. It is just for study and theoretical reference. You cannot expect all your 100 or 1000 employees to be at the same level of performance all the time. Even high-performing people cannot maintain their high performance all the time, there will be vibrations.

To evaluate the real scenario, I conducted an experiment along with my team. We reached out to 8 companies and selected 20 professionals from each including managers and heads of department (HODs). We handed them 3 pages with written English content and asked them to count the number of 'a's on the first page, 'f's on the second, and 'a's again on the third. The time allotted was 75, 60 and 45 seconds for the first page with 290 words, the second page with 310 words, and the third page with 340 words, respectively. The result was what I hypothesized. In all the cases, company managers were less capable of identifying letters than their subordinates! The underlying reason is that managers and HODs overlook things in their day-to-day activities, which makes them less prone to close observations. On the other hand, the people who work on the shop floor like operators and inspectors are more concerned about details. Although they may not know the technical aspects of their work, they will honestly do what you tell them to do.

It was not about the skill but about the system (skill is a consideration but when you evaluate performance look at the system). Humans are emotional objects. As I explained previously, our cognitive vibrations are largely different at different times and we cannot control them. It is how our brains are designed. Nobody can claim that they can maintain their thoughts and work at the same level throughout their working hours. It is impossible. At the same time, this cannot be an excuse to allow errors or defective products to be passed on to your customers.

Then what is the solution? Establish a system. Your employees are committing errors and passing those errors to your customers because your system allows them to do so. Your employees are not solving problems because your system is not asking them to. Your problems are repeating endlessly because your employees are not solving them with the right approach i.e., the systemic approach. Even if you cannot control their psychology, you can structure your system to control their work behaviour and their activities at the work table. This is what my systems psychology research is all about. Though we cannot control people's behaviour directly as we often recruit new faces, we can control their work behaviour through the system. Even though the hands may change, work behaviour will remain the same. That's the advantage of rigid as well as resilient systems.

In the last year, I have used the concept, "When it comes to improvement, quality is a psychology," extensively to improve quality at my suppliers.

A simple test would be to go with the textbook definitions of quality to your shop floor workers and make them understand your theoretical definition. It won't work. Complaints will continue even after having multiple checkpoints. Complexities blind your workers, and unfortunately, you often remain unaware of this problem. When I understood that this psychology was at the centre of quality improvement, I started working on improving the observational skills of the workers at my suppliers. I can prove with the data that I have collated that just clear and calm observations can prevent about 80% of the errors. I have confirmed this aspect even with contractual workmen. The observation-based certainty approach worked well wherever I put it into practice. In some companies, I displayed the following text matter in prominent places.

"I am a calm and confident person. I read the work instructions and understood them. I know I am responsible for my job and its effects. I will not let the company face problems because of errors in my work. I am a member of the team and the success of the company is my success."

I asked the workmen there to read it often. These positive thoughts gave them mental assurance and that forms the core of quality assurance. Many psychological studies have proved that the principles of conditioning (classical and operant) are powerful tools for changing many aspects of behaviour. In one of my recent experiments, I checked how systems respond under forced influences and that gave me a completely new understanding of the intra-relationship between systemic behaviour and its effects on policy resistance. I have not completed my hypotheses and data analysis, hence, the details are not given here. However, applied behaviour analysis is extremely important in systems psychology, just like in the case of human psychology or any other branch of psychology.

Situations influence behaviour

In these days of strong media but weak understanding, playing the blame game is very easy. All day we keep blaming others, for hikes in prices we blame the government for their poor policies, the police for the traffic (for not being present at peak hours to control what we call the 'ants on the road'), industries for climate change, HR for quality complaints and so on. Nobody is ready to accept problems. Everyone thinks that the problems are out there, not in here. If you keep playing this blame game, you'll never reach the end. All you achieve are bad to worse situations without seeing any signs of the best. Professor Lee Ross calls this 'The tendency to blame the person rather than the system' as a fundamental attribution error.

Many times the reality is different. Neither of us is to be blamed, what we need to understand is that whatever problems or errors occurred are because of behavioural influences. These are influenced by the situations, and those are influenced by the system structure. In other words, system structure influences behaviours. It means that the system is continuously influenced by two types of influencers—internal ones like your workmen and external ones like the market and the environment or indirect influencers. When we use the system to solve our problems, it is the perfect solution as you cannot control every influencer directly. As you know, there may be new faces in the company every day. But what you can do is design your system structure considering the 6 basic things. I am reiterating them—company objectives, company culture, people skills, customer profile, society, and environment.

We are a system too and are an integral part of other larger systems such as the world or the company. We know that what influences the system directly influences us and what influences us is what drives our behaviour. To improve conditions and manage situations and behaviours we need to work on systems, not on individual influencers as they will keep changing. This will be further elaborated in the section on situational awareness in the seventh chapter as this can be better understood if you know some important concepts.

How suppliers and customers perceive your company matters most for quality standards

I am from a supplier management background and have worked for over seven years in this profession, visited over 300 suppliers, conducted over 1000 audits (individually or as a team member), investigated over 100 high-level failures, and consulted for over two-dozen clients in product and process development through systemic practices.

I can distil what I have learned from these experiences to these statements, "Do your suppliers see you as a customer? Do your customers treat you with respect and place their confidence in your business for solving problems?" If not, something is seriously missing!

So far in my career, I have worked in the automobile industry. Over the last 2 years, as a full-time systems developer, I have worked with two aerospace product manufacturers, four aluminium hot extruders, and around a dozen other companies such as FMCG and marketing firms. With all my experience in this field, I can say that supplier management is a difficult profession. This is because the breadth and depth of work are enormous. The involvement begins when the designer makes his first iteration of the designed model and stretches even after the project goes obsolete, as this profession needs to handle field failures also. To manage this broader role, such professionals must be well equipped but, especially in countries like India, companies have very little awareness of the importance of supplier management. This lack of awareness makes the task more complex.

In December 2021, to help supplier management professionals, I started a weekly discussion forum. I used to hold an online session for one hour every Saturday. It was titled 'Saturday with Shiva.' I have discontinued it now as I am not able to make time for it due to my busy schedule. Around 300 professionals attended the online event, most of them were regular attendees and approximately 100 were from supplier management. They used to ask me various types of questions and I don't know what they learned but I learned a lot from them.

The central idea of most questions asked during the session was, "How do I manage my professional life with success?"

My one-line answer was, "Become a systems and design thinker."

Whatever role you may have in your career, both these skills will help you achieve success. Whenever I conduct learning sessions, I often talk about how your suppliers perceive you can influence the quality they provide and how your customers view you is deeply relevant to the amount of business they award you and the way they treat you. Instead of being aligned with them, if you show weaknesses, they will take advantage of you and monetize your weaknesses. A majority of companies (non-systemic practitioners) use this blood-sucking model—monetizing others' mistakes. Suppliers monetize customers' mistakes and customers monetize suppliers' mistakes. This happens due to a lack of systems understanding, lack of systems thinking and design thinking, not because of a lack of business skills.

Whenever I go to manage projects at my supplier or my client sites, I carry the image of being the customer or a problem solver. I never let the company's weaknesses pass on to my suppliers, even the company I worked for had multiple weaknesses.

Design thinking helped me immensely to maintain that image. I teach three frameworks for design thinking. I call this aspect the magic of 3 as it keeps it simple and aids in better understanding. I am an engineer who turned to psychology for further project-related studies and research work i.e. Organizational Learning and Systems Psychology. In the last 3 years, I have conducted several formal and informal experiments in schools and companies. I realised that unless we simplify our words we cannot solve complex problems. Some professionals choose to use complex words just to impress the audience. However, in my psychological studies, I have learned that a human mind is a lazy object. It avoids mental effort.

Before teaching anyone, you need to imagine yourself in their shoes or try to see it from their point of view and ask yourself, "Is your explanation simple enough for them to understand?"

Don't think of teaching a concept unless you can explain it in less than a line or a maximum of 3 minutes. I compressed my design thinking learnings in these three frameworks and practised them for more than 3 years. I have also taught them to hundreds of professionals. They are,

- Holy dot concept: Where design thinking lies
- Three approaches to design thinking
- Three stages of design thinking

My purpose in teaching design thinking was to create design thinkers, not designers. You do not need any advanced software skills to become one. Steve Jobs was not a professional designer but expert designers around the world still refer to the products he had designed in the 90s. The difference between a designer and a design thinker is very simple—designers use their skills to design whereas a design thinker uses his thinking to solve complex problems, educate future designers and make systems understanding easier. Without first becoming a design thinker, you cannot thrive as a designer. You can best become a draftsman or a trained designer.

If you want to become a successful professional, learn to simplify things. I think systems thinking and design thinking are one of the best ways to simplify even the most complex things. Through this simplification, you can influence your suppliers and show them that you are an ideal customer for them, not with any documentation (identity card or fancy titles).

One Sunday morning, in January 2021, I received a call from one of my clients. I was in ISKCON that day and was just finishing my early morning programmes and chanting. The client wanted me to come to his site to meet his customer. Almost 6 months ago, there had been a serious complaint from that customer. The complaint had been resolved, actions had been submitted, and it had not recurred in 6 months. Still, every month, 5-6 employees from the customer's end would visit my client at least two times and have a detailed review. However, the customer still had doubts as they were global players so they didn't want to risk their brand. The client wanted me to meet this customer to reassure them as their global team wanted to conduct an onsite review.

I went there and attended the meeting. After that, I called the whole team to discuss the reason for these happenings and the lack of trust shown by the customer. I explained the scenario through an example. The police maintain a list called a rowdy sheet which lists the names of the people in that area who have been involved in criminal or unlawful activities. Whenever there is any unrest in the area or surrounding areas, people in that rowdy sheet become the first suspects for the police. In the same way, customers also maintain a list of high-risk suppliers. If you supply something with one serious defect, then all your activities become suspect.

I suggested a solution to my client in the form of an Innovation Day programme. I said, "It is a one-day event wherein your customers are invited as chief guests and your suppliers are requested to attend as guests." You demonstrate your best practices to the customers so that they understand your business from the first point of reference. This is another way of establishing your intra- and inter-relationships. You can celebrate Innovation Day on your foundation day as the day you established your company is the day you provided innovation to this world. Normally, as customers, we visit our suppliers only when we face any issues. In case there are no problems, we do not carry out regular visits to conserve our resources. Due to this, customers remain blind to the supplier's best practices.

The normal comment when the customer receives a defective piece is, "If I have received a defective product means that the practices you have put in place are not effective."

The suppliers are then demotivated as their ego is depleted and their expertise is criticized. This is what I call an uncertainty approach. In other words, as customers, we make visits to detect uncertainties.

I opined that if, as a supplier, I invite my customers voluntarily and demonstrate the capabilities of my team, our practices, the products we developed, the product profile, technological capability, research ability, suppliers base, and their development plans, our problem-solving ability, plans for the next year, etc. I will be giving my customers a first-hand view of my business. My customers will no longer see me as one of the members of the *rowdy* sheet (high-risk supplier). I will be seen as an innovative supplier and a problem solver.

I always remind each supplier and my clients, "Do not supply products, supply confidence in the shape of products. Create a first point of reference in your customers' minds so that they will place their confidence in you. What you say matters little compared to what you demonstrate and practice."

The concept of the first point of reference works everywhere. It is the image or a picture that comes before your eyes when you think of someone or something. This approach is necessary, be it personal or professional relationships. What others 'see' in you depends on how you 'look' to them.

This approach worked well wherever I recommended it and my clients stated, "It changed our image in the minds of our customers and suppliers."

This first point of reference is what those strategists take months to teach you through personal or company branding techniques. They normally give you dozens of confusing strategies and steps to follow. All those months of lectures can be condensed into the few paragraphs I have mentioned here and just one concept, the first point of reference.

However, later in my research on organizational learning, I changed the pattern of this approach. You will learn more about this in the 6th chapter—the everyday Innovation Day concept.

Change is inevitable, you cannot stop it but if you think your practices are good and you are doing great, do not change yourself, change the way others look at you. No change is sustainable without systems. Look at all the changes that happened in history, only those changes backed by systems have been sustained. The change makers developed a system with 6 basic considerations and made sure that the changes achieved three fundamental characteristics. The rest vanished without making any impact. Normally, we consider stability versus change as an issue. But if we approach it through systemic practices, this conflicted intra-relationship between change and stability can become a path towards sustainability. I won't go into the details of how that happens in this book, however, with careful study of the chapters on organizational learning and systems psychology, you can understand the basics.

Before closing this chapter, I want to mention an example about my concept 'when it comes to improvement quality is a psychology'. This specific instance is taken from the book 'Straight From The Gut' by Jack Welch. During one of his visits to the Yokogawa plant in Japan in the mid-1970s, he mentions how a worker was conducting a quality test of an ultrasound unit.

He says, "When the machines were finished [assembled], a worker unbuttoned his shirt, dabbed some gel on his chest, and ran the ultrasound probes over his body for a quick quality test. The same guy then wrapped up the product, put it in a box, attached a shipping label, and got it on the loading dock."

This is a superb example of my concept, quality is psychology and how to make your systems foolproof by using the intrinsic systems concept. Those quality workers did not just check product quality but also packed and labelled it at the same station. You cannot build and develop this type of culture unless you bring psychological changes to the organization or company. You can never enforce such behaviours, they have to come from the inside—self-motivation, the desire to work systemically.

Chapter 4

Problem Solving

> "If I had an hour to solve a problem, I would spend fifty-five minutes identifying the problem and five minutes solving it."
>
> –Albert Einstein

Most often, problems are not real problems, instead, the methods we use to solve them are the issue.

No matter who you are, no matter what your profession is, you spend your time solving problems. Whether you're a scientist, an engineer, a sanyasi, a politician, an entrepreneur, or just living an ordinary life as husband and wife, you are solving problems. However, how we interpret, interact, and learn depends largely on the approach we follow to solve those problems. The right approach leads to solutions whereas the wrong one leads to negative effects. Over time these become more complex problems. I call the right approach the systemic approach and the wrong one the non-systemic approach.

To make it easy to understand, I have arranged this chapter in the following sequence. First, we will understand the definition of a problem, then move on to a bit of theory, then I will take you through an investigative study, and the learning outcomes from that investigation. I am sure that by the end of this chapter, the way you look at problems will definitely change. This sequence is designed to achieve that.

You can define a problem in multiple ways, but as of now, I will take the definition from CQI-22: Cost of Poor Quality Guide by the Automotive Industry Action Group (AIAG).

- Something is not happening that should be
- Something is happening that should not be

When I write this definition on the board or present it on the screen, I always see lines of confusion on my participants' foreheads. Do not try to understand the whole meaning of those two lines, all you need to understand is one word. That word is 'should.' What does 'should' mean?

You can never know what is not happening unless you know what needs to happen. The word 'should' refers to the requirements—the systemic requirements or in other words, the functional requirements. Since the system does all the work or functions, defining requirements in terms of a systemic way of working gives it a precise direction. In this chapter, I will walk you through two approaches to prevent problems and then tell you about the one that gives better results and how to derive the maximum from the requirements you have defined.

If you ask me, "Mr. Naik, I want to learn only one skill, which skill would you recommend?"

Without thinking twice, my answer would be, "Learn how to solve problems in a systemic way."

You will come across various types of problems demanding different skills throughout your life. This could be in your professional life or your workplace where you spend the majority of your waking and productive hours or your personal life where you spend your time with dear and loved ones.

For this book, I have focussed on professional settings. All of us are surrounded by problem creators and even the solutions we provide create problems because we haven't solved them with the right approach. Without following a systemic approach whatever problems you solve are akin to wrapping the problem in a new cloth. It will hide the smell for a moment or if you are lucky for a year or even a decade, but remember, you haven't solved the problem yet! It will resurface, sooner or later. Let's understand this through case studies.

Let us become problem solvers and investigate a field failure. As we go along whatever I have written till now and will write further in this book can be precisely observed in this investigation.

Case Study: Complaint about a broken aluminium bracket from an Original Equipment Manufacturer (OEM).

Brief: Almost a year ago, one of my clients contacted me to share information about a field failure. An aluminium bracket had broken very severely. We discussed the incident and after the call, I collected some basic information, like the material and its grade, manufacturing process, manufacturer and some photographs of the broken part.

On the evening of the same day, he asked me to join him on a visit to the manufacturer as there were serious signs that the issue will become bigger and if it repeated there may be chances of vehicle recall as well. I joined him with minimal and very raw information.

We asked for an all-function meeting the same day and the manufacturing head arranged it. We shared a failure brief and the meeting ended on a positive note. They decided to run the process the very next day and I went to audit the process as a first step in the investigation.

I took control and the very next day the team ran their process. I did the process audit and stayed there for a couple of days to get the products tested in all possible ways. The results were a bit convincing and with such results, I could not identify the cause of failure. The parts were passing all the design calculations but I refused to give supply clearance as I hadn't found the problem yet.

I told my client's team, "Giving supply clearance without knowing the problem is risky. I don't recommend such a decision. Anyhow, the final call is with you. I can only recommend that you should not give clearance." They agreed and didn't.

I followed my old-fashioned technique by writing on the wall and pasting pictures around. I spent several nights brainstorming over the problem and the days with laboratory tests. All the tests I asked for did not show any problem. Everything was right but the broken bracket (fracture faces) was telling me a different story altogether. I knew there was a serious problem. I always listen to the failed parts, not the people, because it knows what happened whereas the people weren't there.

As a last attempt, I asked for an X-ray test. It is not recommended for extrusion parts. But we did it and there was something in that. The X-ray analysis of the parts showed a sign of inclusion. FMLD or Foreign Material Low Density was reported.

I did my homework and wrote the hypotheses. One big shortfall in this investigation was that we did not have any of the undamaged fracture faces. We lost one portion in the failure, as it had broken down on the road and OEM people damaged the other faces. All we had was a few pictures and the remaining portion of the broken part. If we had fracture faces, we could have done fractography and gotten some more clues about the problem.

Two months later, I made my second visit to resume the investigation. I wanted to know which FMLD it was and test my hypotheses. This time I was prepared when I entered their premises. I knew there was a problem and I was damn sure it was not superficial. I called for trials again and took over complete responsibility. I did not allow anyone to influence the operators. I precisely monitored every parameter and noted the outputs.

I applied my system modelling approach, my favourite tool whenever I study complex problems. As a first step, I marked the relationship between system properties, temperature and pressure. The relationship between T and P was as below,

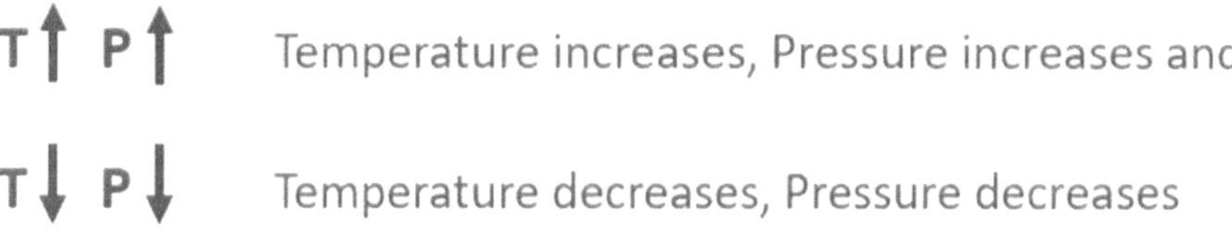

Figure 4.1

The process starts with temperature input through pre-heated metal, hot die and container and pressure is applied through the ram. But when metal reaches the system (here die is the system, it is a product-centred system) both temperature and pressure go out of control because of the thermodynamic work inside the die. Due to friction and thermodynamic work, the temperature inside the system rises while the pressure also increases as shown in the above diagram. It means that the complete system is out of control.

According to system philosophy, any system that is not in control is a dangerous thing, just like a bomb. The bomb is also a system. There is a chemical system for chemical bombs and an atomic system for atomic bombs. Nobody can control the reaction within it.

At that precise moment, we introduce another input i.e. speed, to bring the system back in control. This speed input is a very crucial step. Kindly refer to the system model (Figure 4.2) and you will see that speed goes into the system as a third input and influences it.

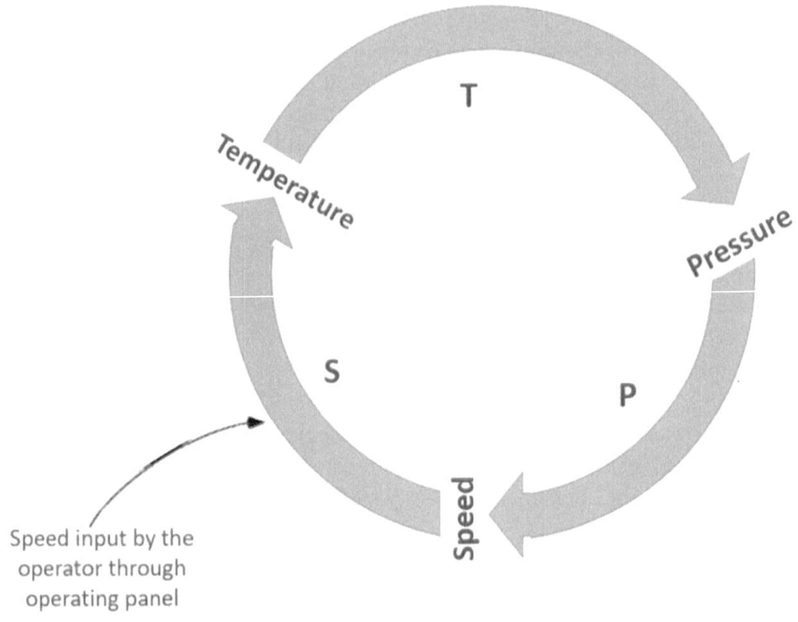

Figure 4.2

In the first trial, I found a defect. Centre cracks or speed cracks, a kind of steps, were observed on the inner surfaces where the die has direct contact with the extruded profile. As depicted in the picture below (Figure 4.3), I found cracks at point A alone and not at point B.

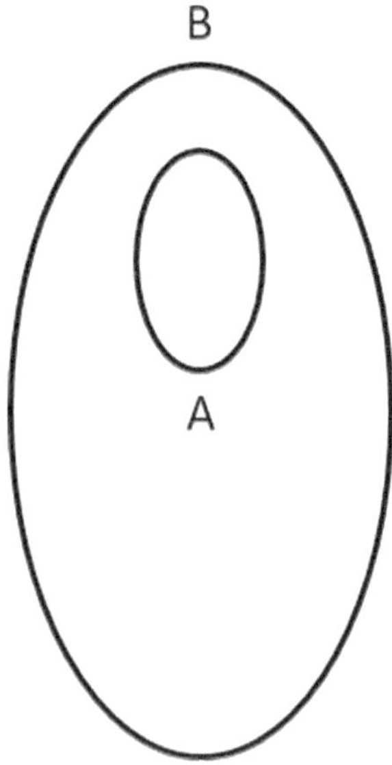

Figure 4.3

To understand this defect, it is necessary to understand how the metal flows while extruding profiles. Point B in the above figure experienced more displacement as compared to point A because of the temperature difference. This difference in material displacement between point A and point B was very critical. If displacement at B was too high compared to A, then stresses develop within the metal. When stresses go beyond the limit, steps like transverse cracks start forming. The industry refers to these defects as speed cracks assuming that they are caused due to the higher speed, but that was not the actual reason. Our systemic study will show that there was something else involved.

Somehow the temperature was exceeding the system's limit or the maximum temperature and stresses that the metal could withstand as the metal was breaking. Thermodynamically, when you heat a metal the force required to move it will increase because it will try to stick to the surface—for the same mass, it requires less force to move a cold body than a hotter body (because of thermal expansion and molecular energy gain). The same thing was happening here as well, though the hot body required more force than the cold body, the supply of force is uniform. This created displacement differences and caused breaking. Observing the speed cracks, I concluded that point A is significantly hotter than point B. But why?

To understand this, I wrote an equilibrium equation referring to the data,

Hi + Temperature rise in the system = Ho,

Hi means temperature/heat input

Ho means temperature/heat output

The equilibrium equation is a very significant factor for any system to work. Though it is called the equilibrium equation, it talks about the potential difference. If you want to keep any system functioning, there has to be a potential difference. If it reaches equilibrium then the system will stall.

For example, what will happen if supply equals demand? The markets will stop functioning, right? Markets are a system wherein sellers and buyers are the influencers, market equilibrium means sellers and buyers are equal and there is no need for the market.

To return to our case study, because of friction under extreme pressure, the temperature was rising and somehow this rise was exceeding the limit, leading to speed cracks. Unfortunately, we cannot measure what's the temperature inside the system as it is deep inside the die.

After making these observations noted, I got some parts tested for the tensile load to see the effect of this defect. It confirmed that speed cracks significantly reduce the mechanical properties and this can be as high as 63% (refer to the Table 4.2 for the relevant data). This was killing the material i.e. if the metal can take 1000 kgf when it is not defective, it fails at just 370 kgf when there is a speed crack. Another indication of dangerously increased temperature was the formation of coarse grains.

After analyzing the pressure graphs of the three products I extruded I found that when the speed input was introduced, the system properties got affected and the relationship between the three variables became as shown below.

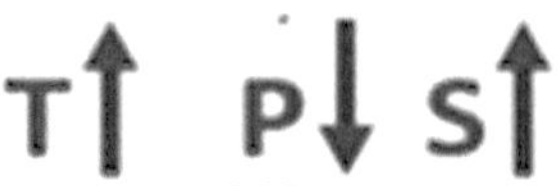

Figure 4.4

Once the equilibrium condition was met or reached negative, which means that the exit temperature was equal to or less than the input temperature, the system entered into a positive feedback loop. This was a vicious cycle as shown below and this began generating defects endlessly. As the temperature increased, the pressure required to displace was reduced and the speed of displacement increased. This increased speed further increased the temperature as work done by the system increased, and so on.

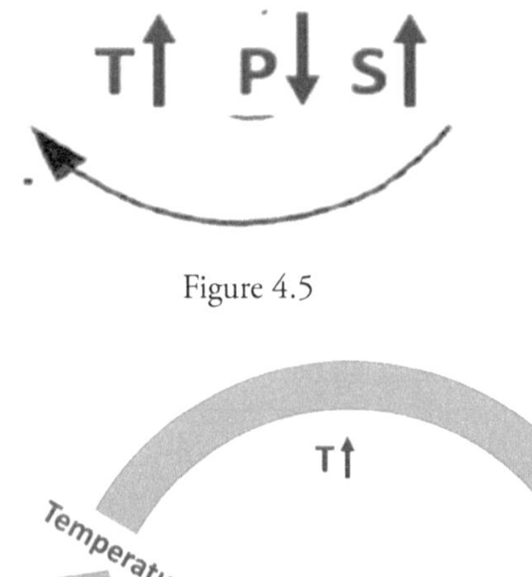

Figure 4.5

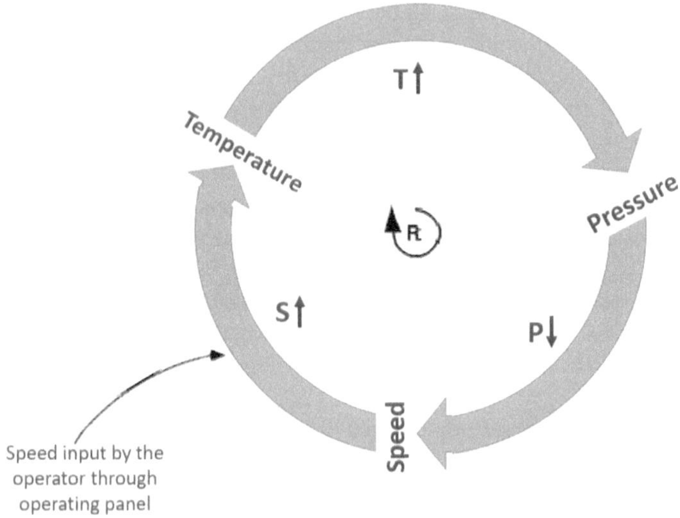

Figure 4.6

One point to be noted in the above relationship (Figures 4.4, 4.5, and 4.6) is that as the pressure decreased the temperature increased. But thermodynamically, the higher the temperature higher the force needed to displace (Figure 4.1). This sounds contradictory, right? But, in the system, this happens very precisely. In my trials, I observed that solid profiles experienced fewer speed cracks than hollow profiles. I extruded 3 profiles, 1 solid (with just 2 holes) and 2 hollow ones (with 6 pockets). The wall thickness played a major role here, by creating a cold body and hot body phenomenon. A significant thickness of the layer sticks to the surface experiencing low velocity or hot body, requiring more force to displace, whereas the majority of the layer experiences ease of sliding, less temperature or cold body, displacing under lesser force. This difference caused jerky motion, which created steps like cracks. Though I had worked on a couple of projects in the last year and successfully solved problems with the same system modelling, I still needed to conduct highly controlled experiments to know how thickness contributes to this displacement difference. I also needed to assess which other factors influenced the crack so that I could model the system and relationships better.[3]

So, was speed crack the problem? No. There was something else. I did not stop. I asked for the next trial. I wanted to know why the speed crack was formed. From the system's point of view, the speed crack was just an extended symptom. However, from the process point of view, it was the problem. But unless I figured out what was wrong in the system, the problem was liable to repeat at any time.

In the next trial, I once again precisely monitored everything. This time I optimized speed and temperature. I got some good material and I played with speed to check if the defects got repeated and they did. The test results were almost similar to those of the earlier trial.

In my hotel room that evening, I sat looking around at all the things I had written on the walls. I studied all the previous data and found that there was an alloy change after the very first trial (during development). However, they had not informed the customer about this change and had not recorded it in their engineering change records either. It was a completely systemic gap (company-centred system). My next question was why did they change the alloy? There had to be a reason for that. After digging through the data and my conversation with people, I came to know that they had faced speed cracks and die pressure issues in the earlier trials. So they changed the alloy, within the same grade, but with a slightly different chemical composition, mainly Chromium (Cr).

	Load Sustenance	Raw Material	Exit Temperature
Failed part batch	3500 kgf	Old	Unknown
First trial	5500 kgf	Old	520 °C
Second trial	9700 kgf	New	515 °C

Table 4.1

With all this information and data, I modelled the system and entered the numbers in the model. It was very clear that the problem was in the system—both the company-

3 Note: At the system level, a positive feedback loop following a different relationship here (may be because of cold body-hot body phenomenon). The pressure decreases as temperature increases. But thermodynamically, pressure increases as temperature increases. To study why this happens, I need some more process data to check how this relationship builds, how it affects the system, and how exactly that positive feedback loop initiates in differently shaped profiles. The data I have is enough to solve this problem and other similar ones but to make it a fitting model more data is required.

centred and product-centred ones. What concerned me was that they didn't even know this. They had been unknowingly running their process for over five decades!

The new system that I modelled looked like the diagram given below.

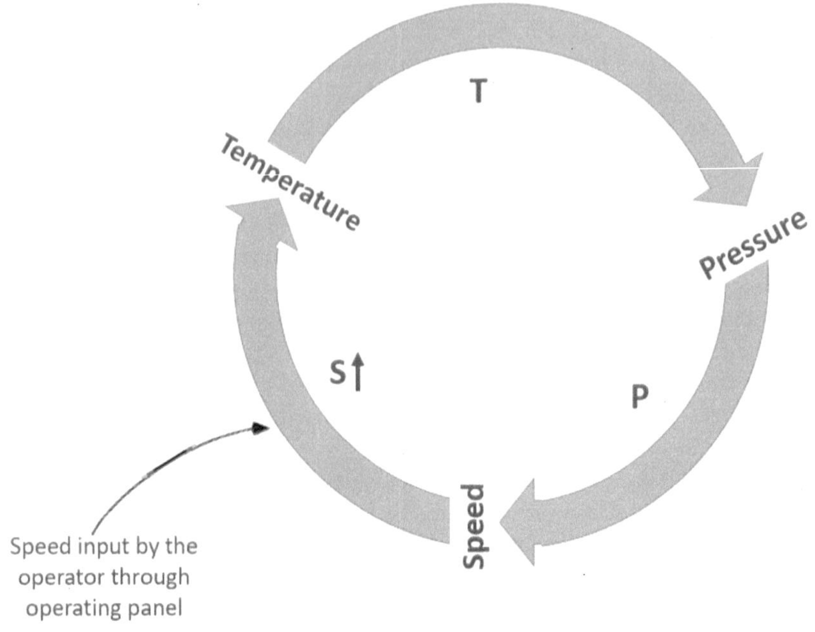

Figure 4.7

Here, I disengaged the temperature and pressure from the external influences and let that into the system's control. By controlling the speed input we should achieve that equilibrium equation. When we successfully achieve that equation of potential difference or when we don't allow the system to reach equilibrium, then it will work reversibly without generating any defects.

I discussed this model with the client and the manufacturer and shared my recommendations to redesign their die, I told them that they could disengage this pressure from the influence through the fusion gap in the die. With the continuous measurement of exit temperature and having precise controls on the speed input, they can disengage temperature from the influences. In the end, they will achieve a fantastic working reversible system that will never generate defects.

To summarize the investigation, it was a company-centred system failure as being a certified company, they had violated validating and recording engineering changes. It was also a product-centred system failure as they used the wrong die design and even after getting repeated speed crack issues, did not bother to study the system.

I could see the coarse grains on the failed part which was a clear indication of a defect directly pointing to the speed crack. I had already tested the speed crack and coarse grains. They could kill strength to the extent of 63%! It was a whopping number! The part broke due to the defective process.

I asked for one more trial to set and optimize process parameters and establish a simple method to test coarse grain structure. The trial went off successfully. I handed over the process parameters to run with and shared some work instructions for coarse grains testing. I also carried some parts for tests at my client's end, just to give them confidence. After the tests, I gave them supply clearance to run the process with the recommended parameters with confidence.

The test results comparison is given in the table below.

Sl. No.	Speed Crack (1st Trial)	OK (3rd Trial)
1	4310	10974
2	4180	9047
3	4510	10918
4	3608	9677
5	4199	9916
6	3943	9334
7	3934	9083
8	4352	9758

Table 4.2

In my final report, I mentioned that the problem was in the system. They had not followed standard practices for engineering change and had the wrong die design. I recommended that the manufacturer should redesign the die. I attached the block diagram (Figure 4.8) in my report to convey that point. Unknowingly, they had designed a high-pressure die that is used for softer alloys. This internal pressure is controlled in the die design by varying the welding chamber or fusion gap. As mentioned in the diagram below, it is almost an imaginary space where metal splits, and then fuses or welds at the next die section. This gap plays an important role since the part that my client was using was for automobile applications. Maintaining these deeper technical things was very important though it does not affect general profile extrusions as much.

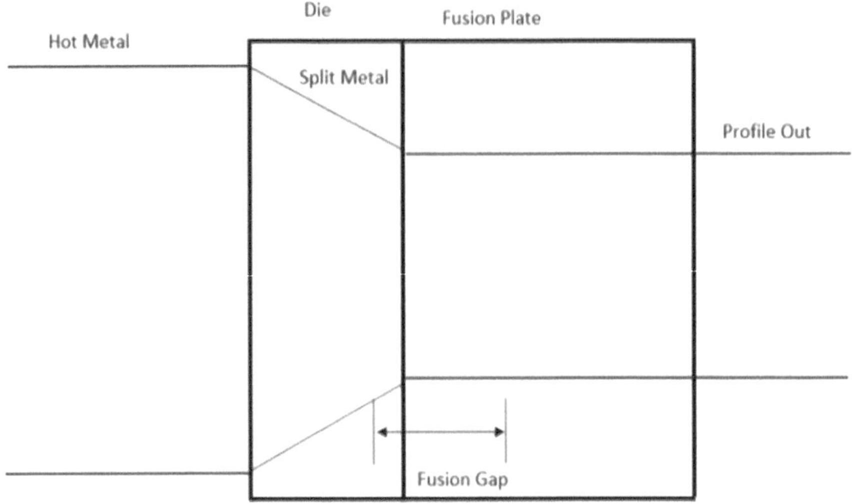

Figure 4.8

Like any major investigation, this one too had begun with more questions than answers. It took me more than a month to find my point of focus. Until then all I knew was that though I had nothing to say, I was sure that something was not right. It is never easy to find out what went wrong when you are handling a major incident. It is not an easy situation to handle. You are under pressure from all sides and everyone wants quick answers. It took me four and a half months to complete this investigation. It changed the entire understanding of one of India's biggest extruders and their global die design partners. I went through over 4000 pages of literature and the total cost of this defect was over two crore Indian rupees.

I did a further investigation at my client's end to know what allowed the manufacturer to change the alloy and why it was not identified there. I found some serious issues at the client's end as well. They had not conveyed their requirements in technical ways. They had just shared the drawing and asked for the product. There were no performance requirements mentioned and nor were the initial parts tested for performance. The assembly process had errors like cross-assembling, deviations were allowed during stages of product development, and product stress analysis was not done appropriately. Though all these are latent errors they become contributors when there's a chain of events.

Over the next chapters, I will draw your attention to how every deviation can poison your system. One psychological issue contributed heavily to this problem. This will definitely be new learning for you. In psychology, we study a very special type of behaviour called escalation of commitment. This is a kind of human behaviour wherein, despite being trapped in negative results, people stick to their decisions and feel a strong need to justify their decisions to others. In this problem too, this escalation of commitment from one of the seniors i.e. a forceful influencer played a crucial role. He allowed deviations and forced the team to bypass tests. Though the decision to develop those products was absolutely right, the way that development was carried out had serious flaws. However, here I want to clarify that I am not talking about a particular person. Since I am from a system practice background, I do not prefer tagging humans for their errors. I'm talking about the behaviour and, in turn, the system.

In my investigation, I found that there were multiple indications that these products are going to fail and the initial event had begun at least a year before the actual failure occurred but nobody had looked at that, which was a complete breach of the systemic approach. Despite initial wrong results, the senior person in charge had gone ahead, approving a couple of deviations just to develop the product and justify his decision. Such people make decisions without considering the risks and even after seeing negative results, stick strongly to their bad decisions to justify them. This is one of the serious psychological issues in workplaces. It is observed mainly in companies where the system is seen in the form of just certifications and compliances. It is not about who is right or who is wrong, what matters is whether the system is right or not. If you study major failures, you'll find that in one way or the other, individual interests played a strong role, just like this one. The forced influencer (senior person) had used situational benefits and ignored signals because the system allowed him to do so. If the company had a strong system, then he wouldn't have had a chance to negatively influence it.

Why have we become blind to such errors?

In every company you go to, majority of the professionals define the problems upfront. As soon as they receive a complaint, the managers ask their team to write the problem statement. This is a very basic practice for those who advocate widely accepted tools like 8D—8 disciplines of the problem-solving methodology. If your first turn is wrong, every turn that follows will be wrong automatically!

On the contrary, I always try to avoid this mistake. I never define the problem upfront. Since a large number of industries practice this methodology, I educate my suppliers about these tools but I never use them for my investigations. The very word 'discipline' is highly confusing. The dictionary meaning is, "the practice of training people to obey rules and orders and punishing them if they do not." But the origin of the word states that it has been taken from the Latin word 'Disciplina,' meaning 'learning.'

I don't know what the people at Ford Motor Company who developed the 8D methodology were thinking. Did they want to train people to follow rules and punish them if they didn't or did they want to educate people?

Whatever their thoughts may be, I oppose the method because of only one reason, "Why do you want your problems to teach you discipline? Can't you be disciplined enough to prevent problems?"

It's not about not solving the problem. I am interested in ensuring that the problem does not originate. That is the reason I placed this chapter here, instead of the beginning. To become a problem solver the first thing is to know the theory of systems. Then, understand the problem, but never be in a hurry to define it. Without understanding the events that led to the problem, don't define it. The last step is to solve the problem and work to prevent it from happening again. Everywhere professionals talk about prevention, but in reality, they don't prevent problems, rather they reinvent problems by following non-systemic approaches.

To ensure that a problem does not originate, you must design a suitable system structure with the help of the 6 basic considerations mentioned earlier. You don't need to train your people for such a system, as you have already considered their skill levels in structure. Training is needed only if you have designed the wrong system. Avoid training and focus on learnings to improve the system continuously.

The right method is right even if nobody is following it whereas the wrong method is wrong even if everybody is following it. The truth is true whether you are aware of it or not. It is everyone's right and responsibility to put in a continuous effort to know the truth and work for the right approach.

Many times the real problem is not the problem itself, but the method we use to solve the problem. The problems with today's widely accepted problem-solving methodologies are as follows.

- They ask you to define the problem up front when you know nothing or hardly know about what happened
- Talk about complexities but no one defines what those complexities mean
- There is a serious gap of neglecting interests, i.e. Needs, Interests, Concerns, and Expectations of stakeholders or interested parties. Unless you know what you require, how can you solve problems?
- Categorization of factors is not considered, which easily masks a lot of factors that can cause a problem
- Stop analysis when they reach some level and tag it as the root cause, however, there is another world beneath the *root*
- Biggest of all, not taking into account the feedback or side-effects of the solutions which you have implemented as PCA or Permanent Corrective Action

Let us discuss these flaws a little more deeply.

- **Ask you to define problems upfront:** My mentor, a renowned behavioural scientist says that in psychology we talk about two types of biases and a heuristic—confirmation bias, desirability bias and availability heuristics. Confirmation bias means seeing what we expect to see or the tendency to get our views confirmed. When this confirmation bias starts to influence our behaviour, it places us in a closed system wherein only the information we believe is processed and the rest, even the most obvious ones are either neglected or ignored. Desirability bias means seeing what we want to see or what we desire to see. Availability heuristics emphasize what comes to mind first or most readily, it is like a mental shortcut.

  If you define what your problem is when you know nothing about it but have just seen a picture or heard something over the phone, you will find what you want to find or what you expect to find either biases or heuristics. In less than a year in my profession, I got fed up with everyday issues. All the issues were repeated. In order to find a permanent solution, I turned to some innovative ways and developed the first version of the four-step problem-solving framework.

I never encourage the practice of defining the problems up-front. You need analysis to find the problem. If you know the problem why do you need to analyze anything? Go and solve it, it's that simple. I completed my Six Sigma Black Belt in 2021. My course guides Pankaj and Shashi cleared all misconceptions in the very first class. They said that any analysis or project you take up demands three resources—time, team, and money—so always ensure that you take up Six Sigma projects only when you don't know the problem. If you know the problem, go ahead and solve the issue. There is no need for analysis using these fancy tools and techniques.

You can take up analysis only when you don't know the problem so that you can identify it or identify the source(s) of the symptoms. Once you know what the problem is, the solution won't take any time. Dig deeper into the problem and you will find your solution.

Identifying any problem takes time. Problems rarely expose themselves at the very beginning. All you see is a symptom and that too a raw symptom. You need to work on that to know the actual symptom. I call this an extended symptom. You can then proceed towards further steps as briefed in the four-step framework.

- **Defining complexities**: None of the methodologies normally discuss systems. Some may ask you about systems indirectly. But why are systems not mentioned directly when systems are everything and they are the ones who do all the work? The usual methods debate with open-ended questions (without any fixed or defined boundaries). Complexity multiplies when we face spatial disorientation. Initially, you were asked to define the problem, now you are asked to analyze the problem but there's no definite direction. You'll be spatially disoriented. This is similar to finding your friend's home in Mumbai without the address. Systems are complex but if you follow a systemic approach, the complexities will resolve themselves.
- **Knowledge about requirements:** Without giving a background about their requirements, many methods directly ask you to delve into what is the underlying problem. Unless you know what you need, how can the problem be analyzed? What is the problem in the first place? The definition clearly states that something is not happening that should be or something is happening that should not be. Here the very word 'should' means the requirement(s) and this needs to be clarified before beginning every problem investigation. I use the NICE framework for this: Needs, Interests, Concerns, and Expectations. When you know NICE, it nearly halves your work.
- **Categorization of factors:** In my framework, I have developed 8 categories of factors but I often use only four types. Firstly, obvious factors—what you'll see immediately or the ones readily visible, etc. For example, failure faces like the one shown in the figure of the bolt given below (Figure 4.9). Secondly, plurative factors i.e. more than one factor are responsible for the problem and all these factors are generated from one source. For example, the extrusion process issue where both temperature and pressure caused the problem. The Swiss cheese

model is a great tool for analyzing plurative factors. Thirdly, shadow factors wherein the problem exists elsewhere but you can detect its shadow. Managerial problems mainly fall into this category. There may be forced influence from the managers or seniors but we blame direct influencers like operators. Fourthly, latent factors, remain in the system but are in an inactive or dormant state and are generally unexposed. However, they become active when certain conditions are met. The Swiss cheese model is again a great tool to analyze this factor. You can see that multiple factors in the extrusion bracket problem also fall into this category—assembly issues, psychological issues, etc.—as they all lay latent in the system until the combinations are met.

Categorization helps pinpoint our analysis. For example, consider the image of a thread-stripped bolt given below which was a part of an investigation that I had conducted last year. As soon as I received the failed bolt sample, I categorized it as an obvious factor and asked for only one test, a micro-hardness test on a 0.3 kg Vickers scale. The problem was decarburization. I audited the process and found some gaps in it along with the raw material.

Figure 4.9

- **Going beyond the root cause:** When you reach the root cause do not think you're done with your analysis. In the example quoted earlier, I had strong evidence to stop my investigation and analysis when I found low strength with a speed crack, but I knew that this low strength was just a symptom or an extended symptom of a broken part. I decided to continue the analysis until I found the systemic problem. This could be directly inside the system or with individual functions, known as intrinsic systems. Sometimes, management decisions may become problems. These types of issues become clearer when you study situational analysis. You know, a tree can have multiple roots spread far and wide, so don't just stop and celebrate when you find one nearest root, study the system and reach the mother root.
- **Taking side-effects into account:** Each and every action we put in place as solutions will have side-effects. You may say you have identified a systemic problem and implemented a solution, but your solutions will get proven only when you study system feedback, and find that they are working well in all

possible scenarios. If the feedback is not considered, you may face problems again. Most of the time such resurfaced problems are greater in severity than the original ones. Studying feedback is the most important part of my four-step problem-solving framework and any systemic approach.

In *Toyota Kata,* the author Mike Rother also highlights the above problems. In the section named "What are the results of working with the action-item list approach?" he mentioned the shortcomings given below:

We are asking the wrong question—it leads us to a scattershot approach

We are jumping to countermeasures too soon—we put all our efforts into shutting off the problem somehow, not solving it

We are not developing our people's capabilities—wrong methods never teach people. The method you use to solve the problems plays an important role in learning.

In his book, Rother also highlights two of my systems psychology concepts—problems always lie in the system and when it comes to improvement, quality is a psychology. He repeatedly mentioned issues with human behaviour in a systemic environment. However, the approach he suggested in dealing with such issues is mainly focused on how Toyota dealt with them. In my work, I talk about improving systems and systemic practices so that you can reap the benefits of generalization and naturalization. I started with a simple question—what came first, tree or seed? To learn systems, you need not join a global organization or go to Japan or the USA. Learning systems is very simple when you approach the subject with conceptual learning. Jumping to, either the conclusion or defining the problem, is strictly prohibited in learning.

This may seem like a difficult process but not if you use a problem-solving sheet. You need to fill only 4 boxes with data. You can use any statistical or analytical tool that you are comfortable with as these four steps are very clear in their meaning, which makes you less prone to making errors. The framework is complete in itself. All you need to understand is how to identify systemic problems. The process is given below—

Identify the system first

Whenever you try to solve any problems, always identify the system first. Before getting your hands dirty, look at it from a distance or a bird's eye view like the external view of the banyan tree that I showed you earlier in the book. The great banyan tree is visible in its entirety from afar and the individual prop roots become visible only if you get closer. What you can see from a distance is not visible when you get closer.

Look at the entire system first and then follow it up with system inputs and how they affect the output. I have given a table in the first chapter (Table 1.1) to show that there are two kinds of systems, organization or company-centred systems and product-centred systems. Systems do the work and all we do is influence the system.

Think about the way a letter that you post in Delhi reaches its destination, for example, Mumbai. You may write a 3-line address ending with the pin code, but until the letter reaches the office mentioned in the pin code, nobody looks at the rest of the address. At each level, only the pincode is important. Only after it reaches the postal office closest to the pincode, does the postman read the address and deliver the letter to the recipient. This is exactly what we should do while solving problems—identify the system that takes us to the problem. Don't jump into writing a problem statement at the beginning. People say do not jump to conclusions but I say that you should not jump to define problems as well. First, work on knowing the system.

Potential difference

A system works only when there is a potential difference. The wind blows, water flows, markets function, and businesses run just because there's a potential difference. In the problem I have given above, I wrote down an equation for the system's function i.e. Hi+Temp.rise=Ho. I found that the system was working only when this equation was being followed. The state of equilibrium means there's zero potential difference and the system will stall. This is one of the three characteristics of the system i.e. self-balancing, the system knows how to balance itself. Do not try to balance the system by artificial intervention. Understanding how this potential difference works is of the utmost importance in system modelling. You spend money to buy something. Here too there is a potential difference, the seller has something to sell that you want to buy.

If you design the system as I mentioned earlier, it has a self-balancing characteristic in its structure. You don't need to balance the system by artificial intervention. If you want to understand how the system works, then identify the potential difference. Though there are various ways to do this, the easiest way, which I follow often, is system modelling (I have explained this below).

Four step approach

The four steps include:

- Symptom(s)
- Concern(s)
- Problem(s)
- Cause/Solution

Symptom: The broken bracket is not the problem, it is just a symptom of an underlying problem(s). Since the part has no function, how can there be problems with it? It seems obvious, right? Since the system has a function, there have to be problems in the system. This can be either in the vehicle or the manufacturing process. How do you shortlist these issues? These aspects become clearer when you do a preliminary investigation of the observed symptom. After conducting all possible tests I could have asked my client to deny the concern as everything seemed okay. We had relevant reports too. If this had been our stand, then the vehicle would have been the problematic system. But, after conducting another test, I realised that there was something abnormal in the part. Yes, abnormality and uncertainty in the part are possible as these are the outputs of problematic systems. That took me to the manufacturing process for the second time.

Concern: Once you verified the symptom, it is time to set boundaries for your analysis. You cannot reinvent the wheel, you cannot test everything and every process. You need to set the boundaries for your study. In the above case, the areas of concern were the manufacturing process as I had seen abnormalities in the part and the assembly process as I had seen some parts with tilted assembly. Setting these boundaries further reduces the areas of work and helps in focusing resources. This step is very crucial and it needs to be done carefully. If you select the wrong area of concern, then you will be misguided and if you select multiple areas you'll waste resources, time and money. So, do your homework properly.

Problem: When you set boundaries for the analysis, you need to focus on regenerating the situation by providing the system with various combinations of input to observe the feedback given by it.[4] Precise monitoring is very important at this step as some problems are too complex and will not expose themselves easily. In complex cases, such as the one outlined earlier, there may be no obvious factors, only plural and shadow factors along with a series of latent factors that are waiting for the right combination to become active.

Cause/solution: I don't use the word 'root cause' in my framework and I have also merged both cause and solution since once you find the systemic problem, you don't need to put in any extra effort to find cause or solution. Just dig deeper into the problem to find the solution. What does the doctor do after he comes to know about the problem or disease you are suffering from? He gives medicines. The doctor prescribes tests based on your symptoms and then zeroes in the area of concern. For example, the doctor would not recommend a full body scan every time you go to him/her. Specific tests are conducted and upon receiving the results, the doctor will understand the problem and recommend treatment. If he/she finds something abnormal, like I found the speed crack, some more tests will be recommended for further clarity. Once the precise problem is detected, without going into further analysis, he/she will prescribe appropriate medicines.

The beauty of the four-step problem-solving framework is that you can use it to analyze and solve any problem, whether it's related to your business like that of extrusion case study or general problems like the Coronavirus pandemic (I have discussed this in the next chapter). While selecting words or questions to ask, I ensured that it was built with generalization and naturalization.

I have provided the problem-solving sheet filled with the analysis for both the parts I have mentioned in the section i.e. aluminium bracket (Figure 4.10) and bolt (Figure 4.11) below.

4 Refer to System Modelling section given below to know how to regenerate the situation

Aluminium bracket failure

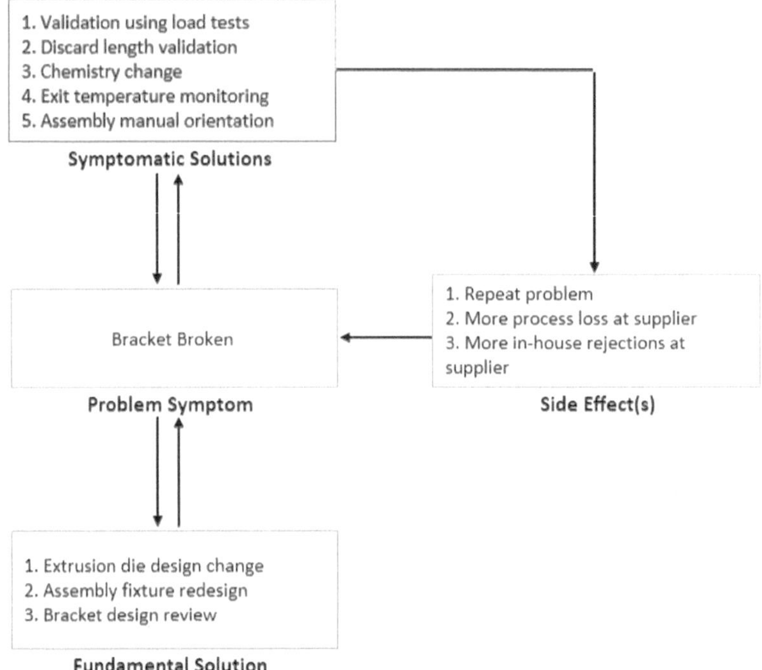

NICE Analysis	
Needs	High strength bracket as per material mechanical properties
Interests	Economics of operation, brackets as per drawing
Concerns	Supplier process and assembly process
Expectations	No complaints from customer & no in-house rejections

Four-Step Framework	
Symptom(s)	Broken bracket (extended symptoms--tilted assembly, speed crack in process)
Concern(s)	Supplier process, assembly process
Problem(s)	Wrong extrusion die design, wrong assembly fixture design
Cause/Solution	Redesign extrusion die and assembly fixture

Figure 4.10

Bolt failure

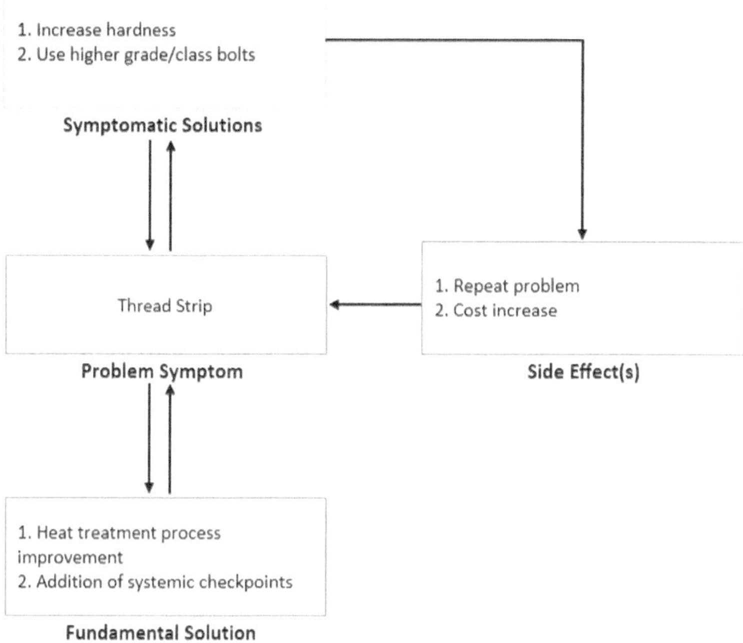

NICE Analysis	
Needs	High strength bolts as per designed mechanical properties
Interests	Economics of operation, bolts as per drawing
Concerns	Supplier heat treatment process, raw material
Expectations	No complaints from customer & no in-house rejections

Four-Step Framework	
Symptom(s)	Bolt thread slip (extended symptoms--low hardness)
Concern(s)	Supplier heat treatment process, raw material
Problem(s)	Decarburization--loss of carbon on the surface
Cause/Solution	Monitor heat treatment process and add systemic checkpoints for regular inspection

Figure 4.11

Problem-solving is an essential skill in the 21st century. From climate change to protests against government policies, from economic downturns to quality issues in industries, one skill is in great demand across the world i.e. solving complex problems. How you solve your problems shows your understanding of the job at hand. The better the understanding, the better you are at it.

If you know how to solve problems through the systemic approach, you'll love the process. You'll never get frustrated and will never avoid problems. In fact, I pray for problems so that I can solve them and find ways to strengthen the system and share the learnings with others. My purpose is to learn and help others in their learning journey. Only complex problems can test your true ability. Don't expect life to be simple, rather prepare yourself to make it simple so that you'll never break down when you are faced with complexities.

Dr. Kalam used to say that handling success is easy, but the true test of your leadership is how you handle failures. The true test of your problem-solving skills is how you handle complex problems while still sporting a smile. You can gain a new understanding with every new problem. Prepare yourself for the worst as the best is easy to deal with.

System modelling

I didn't write strategies to teach systems instead I developed concepts to teach systems structure. Conceptualization is the scientific way to teach any subject and this is also the way our mind accepts information. To solve problems you don't have to be an expert in that particular field, all you need to know is what concepts drive that particular process or field. This conceptualization thinking is what we should learn during our school or college education. In this book, I will go one step further and reveal how conceptualization helps in solving problems. In this section, I want to discuss system modelling. If you want to know everything then learn how to think in systems. If you know systems, you'll know everything and solve any problem.

Akash introduced me to systems modelling. The words he had written in the notes are somewhat similar to what I found in the book 'Thinking in Systems' by Donella Meadows, a pioneer in the systems thinking world. She says, "There is a problem in discussing systems only with words. Words and sentences must, by necessity, come only one at a time in linear, logical order. Systems happen all at once. They are connected not just in one direction, but in many directions simultaneously."

The purpose of system modelling is to conceptualize system structure and study the behaviours to understand various relationships. Modelling also helps us regenerate the event that led the system to erroneous behaviours. It's like a conceptual representation of relationships of the system's inner workings. Even in the non-systemic approach, people often recreate defects to validate the cause so that they can establish a cause-and-effect relationship. However, this approach has at least two flaws.

First, a cause-and-effect relationship is not always linear. System researchers conducted various studies and proved—especially in the case of complex situations where multiple factors affect the system—that the cause-and-effect relationship is non-linear and could easily divert the system to an erroneous behaviour. In more complex situations, the latent factors go on building within the system which could easily mask our attention.

The second obvious flaw is that if you recreate the effect without understanding the system's behaviour then there are huge chances of ignoring or neglecting feedback or ignoring some latent factors which could lead to failure—either immediately or later.

So, in the systemic approach, we recommend conceptualization through modelling the system instead of mapping linear cause-and-effect relationships, so that you can provide better solutions and, more importantly, learn things. When it comes to solving problems, what you learn is more important than solving problems. Give priority to your learning. That's what I talk about in the learning influencer programme, and that's the beauty of systems psychology.

Problem prevention

Let us now discuss problem prevention. There are two approaches to prevent the occurrence of problems:

- Certainty approach: Focus on what you require
- Uncertainty approach: Focus on what you do not require

Certainty approach

Describing or stating your requirements and checking their alignment with the actual is what I call the certainty approach. Being a systems thinker means that you are a follower of this approach. Describing and conveying what I need is much easier than describing what I don't need. In the above case study, my clients didn't convey their needs in an understandable form. They thought that since they had shared the drawing, the engineers employed by the manufacturer would be able to easily read and understand the drawing. However, they did not include the performance requirements on the drawing explicitly. The material grade was mentioned on it, which indirectly refers to requirements, but you must remember that monetizing others' errors is the fundamental way of business. Customers monetize suppliers' errors and suppliers monetize customers' errors. The public monetizes the gaps in government policy and the police monetize strict regulations. This situation exists everywhere. When any serious failure occurs, each party prioritizes escaping from the shackle. After they have found a way to escape, they talk about delving into the problem. I have seen this blame game happening in almost every investigation that I have conducted. This happens mainly because the requirements have not been communicated adequately. This involves not just sending emails or getting signed documents, but taking the onus to ensure that the other party has understood and aligned their system with your requirements.

I always use the certainty approach and ensure that my suppliers understand what I need. This approach cuts the process short significantly and clears the clutter easily. For example, I will make a list of what I need such as I want this product in this dimensional specification, it should be black coated, it has to pass these performance tests and needs to be packed this way, and other specifications. Anything other than those requirements (which affect the quality) is uncertain. Listing what you want is easier than what you don't. Saying that I want this product to be made of aluminium is much easier than listing all the materials from the periodic table which I don't want it to be made of.

Uncertainty approach

Describing or stating what you don't need and checking alignment with the actual offering. In 'The Invisible Gorilla,' authors Christopher Chabris and Daniel Simons demonstrated how our deep focus on some mental tasks makes us blind to even obvious observations. This demonstration is an indication for those who follow the uncertainty approach. You may display defect alerts on work tables but do you know the problem it creates? It makes the workers working there blind to other observations. They deeply focus on the displayed defects and effectively become blind to others. I faced many such instances from my suppliers.

Most companies follow both approaches—their worktables contain standard operating procedures or SOPs which talk about certainty and large photos of defective samples which refer to uncertainty. It creates confusion and an illusion in the minds of the workers (like in the case of the invisible gorilla demonstration). Firstly, they are not as well educated as the person who prepared those papers and put them on display. Secondly, even if they are displayed in the local language, they don't have time to read and understand them. This means what you have displayed holds no relevance for them. The real systemic approach includes how you educate them and what provisions or defences you have built into your system to manage the influence points. In some of the organizations where I worked, I asked them to keep work tables completely blank. I told them to let their defences and systems work and not influence them negatively. Don't just ensure compliance. Displaying SOPs and photographs of defects is contradictory. You just do such things to make your customers happy by showing that you are compliant but that doesn't make your systems happy.

Preventing problems requires certain basic practices

- **Company level uniformity**: Decide the one thing that you will follow throughout, from the security gate to the toilet cleaning checklist, from the display in the director's cabin to the workers' tables. There has to be uniformity and it is good if this uniformity is free of words—be it local, national or international. My experiments have proved it repeatedly. The effectiveness increases if your workers' reference documents are free of words (or with a bare minimum of words if they cannot be completely eliminated). Your workers should understand them just by glancing over them. You can use colour markings, symbols, signage, etc. but what you use in one place has to be used everywhere. Uniformity clears the clutter and avoids confusion. Great systems have to be extremely simple.
- **Put checks on influence points**: Influence points mean the moments or the points where the system comes into contact with people, the influencers. This can be easily understood by the figure given below. Here the system means the organization-centred or product-centred or any intrinsic system like manufacturing booths, quality checkpoints, packaging stations, loading docks, etc. For example, managers pressurize supervisors, and supervisors pressurize workers. These pressures create abnormal situations. You already know that situations influence behaviours and behaviours influence the system. So, controlling influence points is a systemic necessity for achieving effectiveness as well as efficiency. Influences are of two types, natural and forced influence. A description of these will be given in detail in the Swiss cheese model at the end of this book.

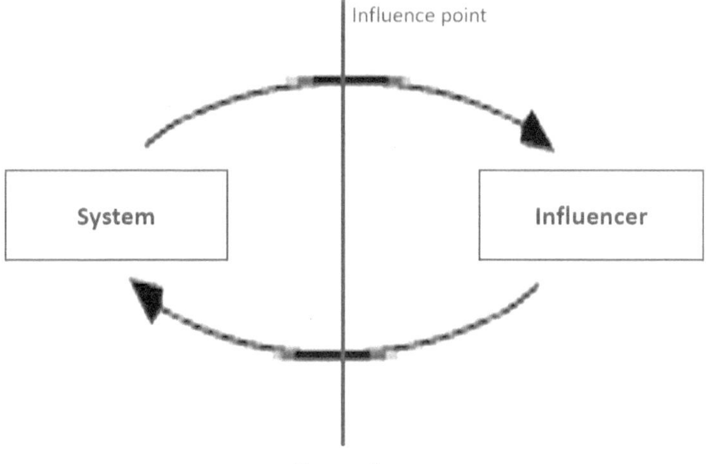

Figure 4.12

- **Understand the priority, effectiveness comes first and efficiency follows**: One booth may manufacture 1000 products in one hour with a 15% rejection rate while another may manufacture 700 products with just a 3% rejection rate. When you calculate overall effectiveness, that of the first and second booths is 85% and 97%, respectively, even when the total products manufactured are fewer by 30% in the latter. Hence effectiveness is given priority. Doing the wrong work faster doesn't reward you.
- **System loves servant leadership**: Authoritarianism doesn't work in systemic environments. Especially if you want to become an organization, you have to adopt servant leadership. A lean and flat management structure is recommended for systemic culture. The leaner the management, the lesser the influencers and the better the working of the system. However, if you have structured the system as I recommended earlier, your management doesn't have much work to do, it is self-maintaining.

Differentiating between leadership and management is a fashion in almost every business book, but in my studies and experiments with systems, I have found a major flaw in this approach. Many of the managers act like dictators. I have listed a few of the important differences between them from a systemic point of view. By hiring incapable managers and giving them responsibilities beyond their sphere of influence, companies push them towards dictatorship. Individual capability packed with the personal sphere of influence helps an ordinary person to do extraordinary acts and makes him/her a real leader.

Differences between leadership and dictatorship:

Leadership	Dictatorship
Believe and follow the servant style of leadership	Believe and follow authoritarianism
Listen, understand, think, and then speak	They speak first and work to enforce their words
Openly welcome feedback and accept suggestions from other team members—open cycle	Don't accept suggestions and do not consult anyone for their decisions—closed cycle
Systems can be built and developed only in leadership cultures	Force influence grows in a dictatorship, systems can never be built
Learning oriented	Depends on training(s)
Creative people love to work with leaders	Intelligent people never like to work under dictators
Treat others as team members—taking others 'with' them	Treat others as if they are 'below' them so that they can prove their authority
Accept responsibility and use personal influence to get things done	Use positional power (authority) to force influence to get things done
Works on long-term vision and holistic growth or sustainability	Focus on short-term gains and personal growth

Table 4.3

- **Move from training culture to learning culture**: I will talk extensively about this in the chapter on organizational learning. As of now, just understand that training creates dependency whereas learning builds confidence. We need to foster confidence to remove dependency. In a systemic culture, learning thrives.
- **Provide freedom to problem solvers**: The first responsibility of a boss is to ensure that there are no obstacles in his/her subordinate's path. Clear the traffic.

One participant told me, "Sir, whenever I try to implement learnings, I face resistance from my boss. What to do? I am learning new things but am unable to implement them."

I didn't know how to answer him. How can I control his boss? I just told him, "I know that this is a big problem. Not only you but even I have faced the same resistance during my initial days. Anyways, I am working hard and fast to solve this problem."

There is resistance everywhere. There are dozens of reasons why we face resistance from our bosses. The 3 main reasons include 'save the seat' campaign, workplace politics, and the normal habits of some bosses. Instead of clearing traffic, they become the biggest roadblock.

If you are also one of the victims, don't worry, you are not alone. I also faced resistance but less in proportion than many others. After some initial resistance, I got bosses who gave me the freedom to run at my speed. They knew that I was capable of solving problems. Except for a few occasions, they always cleared traffic in my path so that I could learn.

That early freedom provided me with opportunities that many unfortunately miss. Not just you and I, but every great personality in history has faced resistance and that became their motivation to create history.

Out of frustration, Swami Vivekananda in one of his lectures said, "If you can solve problems and you want to solve them, then come and solve. Otherwise, leave the road clear, and let others come and solve them. Do not create a blockage."

My suggestion to those who face such resistance is to not fear it. It is everywhere and will exist forever. Keep learning and keep doing good work. Your voice will be heard soon. Good work always wins, sometimes it may be delayed but believe in yourself. This delay in reaching your goal makes you better at it i.e. the later your success the more updated or better you are.

My request to bosses, managers, and management is, "Please give your team the freedom they need and clear the traffic for them. We have problems everywhere but unfortunately, problem solvers are very rare. Let them solve the problems. Who knows, your survival may be in their hands."

Lee Iacocca, the famous American automobile executive who led both Ford Motor Company and Chrysler Corporation said, "I hire people brighter than me and then I get out of their way."

Motivation and demotivation

The subject of motivation is huge if I go through scientific theories, but I will focus only on the essence here. Motivation is a completely internal process, we can divide this into two types—self-motivation and artificial motivation.

Self-motivation means getting motivated from within. It happens when your interests and the opportunities to pursue those interests coincide. Self-motivation inspires you to work on your interests.

Artificial motivation is when you expect others to motivate you. It is a well-known fact that often we don't know what to do in life—you may not have identified your interests, or someone might have hurt you or you may feel sad about yourself. In such instances, you need a dose of energy to regain your self-motivation. You will find thousands of channels and millions of videos on social media platforms to motivate you artificially.

My main objective here is not to motivate you but rather to protect that motivation. As of now, I am not a motivational speaker and don't know if I ever will be in the future. Self-motivation is a highly demanded and respected quality which we expect from everyone, from our parents and teachers to our employers. Identify your goal in life and find opportunities to realize that goal. If you have a goal and you have opportunities to realize it, then you are a self-motivated soul. If you don't know what to do, I recommend the best approach that I followed and still follow is to read good books.

Once you have identified what you want to do in life, follow the earlier path and find opportunities. This is the organic way of getting motivated. Getting motivation from others is also good but it is not an organic way. If you expect others to keep you motivated, it means that you are lacking something in life. Find that something as quickly as you can. Even in criminal investigations, investigators and lawyers always work on finding the motives and opportunities of suspects so that they can present the same before the law and ask for prosecution. Without motives and opportunities, we cannot do anything significant.

So how do you protect yourself from getting demotivated? Motivation is always direct. You can feel a refreshing energy when you get motivated and even if you work long hours you don't get tired by working on a project or something in which you have a genuine interest. You can feel this directly whereas demotivation is always indirect. We don't even notice we are getting demotivated. You join a company fresh out of college, where there's no system or at the minimum, some basic practices of a system. No matter what you try to do, it is resisted by your seniors or boss. You then just start to accept that this is the reality and try to mould yourself to the situation. In just a few months or years, you lose all the motivation you had. When you joined, you thought you would achieve something and you wanted to change things but the situation was different. Every day you may hear from your colleagues or friends that what you learned in college doesn't help in reality. You need to accept the reality and adjust yourself. This attitude of adjusting yourself kills your intelligence as you can see that it has no value. This is how we become machines for others to play with rather than becoming intelligent and self-motivated.

Motivation is an internal state of mind. Many psychologists advise against making scientific statements about motivation. That's the reason it is being studied through observable behaviours. Here too I refer to them. If someone wants to demotivate you, he first needs to deplete your ego through his actions or words. After listening to a motivational story, you get charged and think that you want to do many things so that you can change the world. When you start studying along those lines, your studies make you a little egoistic.

In this respect, having self-respect is good but becoming egoistic (false ego) is really bad. When someone comes to you and says, "You don't do that, you don't know this" and uses all negative words to kill your positivity, your ego gets depleted and you get demotivated. This is what the participant in my session, Suresh, had asked me in Pune. His boss was trying to deplete his ego but Suresh had a strong disposition and didn't want to give up. This desire to keep going without giving up is a great defence against demotivation. My advice to you is to never allow yourself to get demotivated. If you hear something that is making you feel bad or trying to deplete your ego, just walk away. Don't scream at anyone. Try to be self-motivated by finding your goal in life and if you are still confused about your goal, then go for the organic way of getting motivated.

I have explained this in very ordinary language to keep things simple. If you want to learn more about the depletion of the ego, I recommend the research of psychologist Roy Baumeister and his team. They have done immense work on this topic, published in the paper 'Ego Depletion: Is the Active Self a Limited Resource?'

Find your motivation and never let others deplete your ego and demotivate you. Don't take people seriously. Follow only what your mentors say, they know you better than anyone, sometimes even better than your parents.

Another example is from cricket. In cricket, sledging is one such instance wherein one player tries to weaken the opposing player's performance. It is an example of demotivation, but try to connect the dots here. How is that demotivation happening? The motivation of the players is to win the game for their country. The opposing team cannot scold the nation as it will stir the general public, instead, they will use insulting words about the player's style or something else to hurt his ego and make him prone to committing errors. They will then capitalize on the error to win the game. Motivation is direct like winning for the country, but demotivation is indirect and works by depleting the ego or hurting it.

I cannot do what I am doing today without self-motivation. How do I keep myself motivated? If someone tries to deplete my ego by talking negatively about my work, my approach, or anything that I do, I just walk away. I don't say anything to them and I don't stay there, be it a meeting or any casual discussion. I don't mind who that person is, I walk away. In fact, in my seven years of professional career, I changed two jobs for the same reason. People across all levels in both companies were just gossiping about someone's methods and knowledge. They had never done anything worthwhile in their entire career but spent their time gossiping. When they started gossiping about my work, I just quit. You need to know what you are doing and be very clear about your purpose—begin with the end in mind. This is the second among Stephen Covey's seven habits.

I always follow this thought, "Don't try to create your existence; create impact." Existence only gives the feeling as long as you exist, but impact keeps you alive long after you are gone. All great personalities not only existed but also created an impact on the world. That's the reason why we feel their existence even when they are gone.

Ego and false ego

Ego has two definitions. The first is the consciousness of your own identity and the second refers to an inflated feeling of superiority over others.

I refer to the first one as the 'good ego.' It's not bad to be self-aware. You should know who you are. But I consider the second definition as 'false ego,' which makes you feel falsely inflated. Never think for even a moment that you are superior to others. Having an ego is not bad. Unless you have one, you cannot become a teacher and cannot solve any problems. You should be aware of what you know. Being self-aware, you should also understand your weaknesses which leads you to learn.

In psychological settings, we study one more kind of ego called the superego i.e. the conscience. It's a kind of unconscious motivation. By nature, we all are honest and genuine. Though no research has been conducted, this superego is like the nature of children. They are honest and free from any polluted behaviours and thoughts. This is one of the reasons why I recommend thinking like a three-year-old to tap our generative intelligence (this will be described in chapter 6) and use the power of the superego to learn, work, and teach.

Every non-systemic solution incurs a debt to the systems. If you want to work on problems with the wrong method i.e. in non-systemic ways, you will have to do this every time as your problems will repeat endlessly. If you work on just a few problems in a systemic way, you'll be able to solve all the problems at their first appearance. Simultaneously, you will be able to build an excellent system with the 3 fundamental characteristics, a system that maintains, sustains, and balances itself.

Just like knowledge without humbleness is of no use, all your experience, fancy titles, and certifications are of no value if you can't solve problems. Your ability to solve problems is what matters at the end of the day.

Chapter 5

Intrinsic System

We have seen most of the basic things about this topic already. You know what the intrinsic systems concept is all about, and you also know how this concept is different from the whole systemic approach. I will go into some depth in this chapter to help you understand why this concept makes sense and why we need to understand it even after understanding the systemic approach, and many other such queries.

I have three influencers behind developing the concept of the intrinsic system:

- First, Chaitanya Mahaprabhu's achintya-bheda-abheda-tattva is the sublime doctrine of simultaneous oneness and difference.
- Second is the great banyan tree, an individual subsystem that exists and can even take care of the whole system if its structure is designed to the system's objectives.
- Third is the mutually exclusive and collectively exhaustive (MECE) framework of problem-solving.

As you must have observed, the first is the spiritual reference, the second is the general reference, and the third is a business reference. We have discussed the first two influencers in the previous chapters. I will go to the third one directly.

In my 6 years of research journey on systems, the MECE framework was the only one that came close to systems thinking. Some may attach the strategy nameplate to this framework but if you see it through the systems eye, you can see that it is a fantastic way of thinking from the systems perspective. MECE was developed by Barbara Minto, a 1963 Harvard graduate who worked at McKinsey & Company for 10 years and developed this amazing way of solving problems during her tenure there.

In 'The McKinsey Way,' author Ethan Rasiel writes, "Ask any number of McKinsey alumni what they remember most about the way the Firm solves problems and they will tell you, 'MECE, MECE, MECE'."

Like MECE, the intrinsic systems concept also asks you to see things with minimal confusion and hence, maximum clarity. The only difference between them is that MECE looks at problems in highly generic ways whereas the intrinsic system speaks about a systemic way of finding and solving problems. Even if you apply MECE, you would go through a long journey and finally arrive at the systems as real problems can occur only there. Initially, I too used the MECE framework but then realised that it's a longer approach to the same destination so I switched to the more direct intrinsic systems method. The systems way of thinking, systems way of working, and solving problems is always the shortest, safest and most effective way.

In 2014, during my initial conversations, my spiritual mentor Garudadhvaja Dasa from ISKCON Hubballi told me, "Shivalingesha, our philosophy is bheda abheda tattva. The doctrine of simultaneous oneness and difference." This was deeply ingrained in me when I began my research work on systems. While working on simplifying concepts for general understanding, that philosophy and the words of my spiritual mentor helped me immensely.

When you study things in terms of intrinsic systems, you can analyze both intra and inter-relationships better.

Two types of systems and intrinsic systems

Organization Centred System	Product Centred System
Management	Tool, Die, Machine
Accounts & Finance	Production Process
Manufacturing	Handling
Maintenance	Work-in-Progress (WIP) Storage
Quality	Inspection
Purchase	Packaging
Human Resources (HR)	Finished Goods (FG) Handling
Marketing	Finished Goods (FG) Storage
Customer Services	Shipping

Table 5.1

The table above has already been explained in the first chapter (Table 1.1) It shows the two types of systems. Every system manual mainly discusses the quality-centred system or quality management system (QMS) but not solving problems in systemic ways. Most of them do not simplify systemic concepts for wider use. That's the reason why even companies having multiple certifications get stuck in the non-systemic trap and seek the help of strategists to run their companies.

No matter what industry you are in, what products you manufacture, and what services you provide, from barber to banks, from airports to aerospace, from software services to software developers, from taxi services to vehicle manufacturers, all businesses have two kinds of systems—company-centred and product-centred systems. Companies like Facebook and Amazon are also product-based companies and companies like Oracle and Salesforce which offer Software as a Service (SaaS) also have two types of systems.

In an organization or company-centred system, the organization or company is the whole system and individual functions or departments are its intrinsic systems.

In product-centred systems, the production process where the actual product gets formed is the main system and its supporting processes or process steps are its intrinsic systems.

Understanding the intrinsic systems concept helps us focus resources and gets us to the problem quickly. In the four-step problem-solving framework, the second step talks about concerns. This means a focused area or process or function or department you need to identify and direct your resources and efforts to so that you avoid the 'efforts scattering effect' and don't get lost in spatial disorientation. Don't reinvent the wheel. Whatever problem you might be solving, whether it's highly complex or simple, whatever organization you are working for, whether it's a start-up or the government, everywhere you will face constraints, which can be in the form of money, people, and time. Nobody is going to pay you handsomely for inadequate problem-solving skills. A real problem solver works within the constraints and yet delivers extraordinary solutions at lightning-fast speed with no additional people involved. If you know how to simplify things, then you don't require additional resources. Accept your constraints and identify the area of focus where you can concentrate your efforts.

As I mentioned earlier, Akash cautioned me in 2011 when I was just 21 and said, "If you ever want to work with a team, make sure the entire team shares equal competency, otherwise less competent members will negatively influence the team and divert its focus. If you believe this is the solution and have a strong backup and they (especially the higher authorities) don't agree with your methods, then don't involve them. Their influence means a lot, negative influence can have negative results whereas a positive influence can have a positive impact." I never knew that one day his words were going to be my mantra and a unique way to solve problems.

In my systemic approach, I call this forced influence or conflicted influence. When there are conflicted influences or a conflict of interests, the forced influence prevails because it always comes from the higher authorities or indirect influencers. You cannot ignore them unless you are a daredevil. Most of the time in my professional career I went against all the seniors just to show them that this was the easiest way to solve problems. Some thought that I was trying to prove them wrong but honestly, I always focused on solving problems and teaching people. When it comes to solving problems, it doesn't matter who is right or wrong. What matters is whether the problem is solved or not and whether it is solved within the given constraints. If yes, don't care about what others say, go ahead.

Less competent people always try to teach and judge the more competent ones because they want to be listened to. But the truth is, they can never teach. Their voice will only be heard, not listened to.

Intrinsic system thinkers are not reductionists

There's a huge difference between a sculptor breaking a stone and an ordinary person breaking a stone. A sculptor knows how to use his chisel and hammer, the amount of force to apply and how to break the stone whereas an ordinary person will hit it randomly. The sculptors know how to break stones and make beautiful deities that give people joy. The difference between analyzing systems through the intrinsic systems concept and the reductionist approach is similar. Intrinsic system thinkers are like expert divers. They solve problems by diving deep into them to make our lives easier and our world more meaningful.

Reductionists are the ones who break things into bite-sized pieces just for easier understanding but doing so makes learners of this approach blind to many of the factors I mentioned in the problem-solving chapter. Missing even a single factor can easily take us towards an erroneous solution or not help in finding the problems at all. Psychologists distinguish between two types of blindness—the absence of eyesight (gross blindness) and being blinded due to our illusion or false beliefs or inattentiveness (subtle blindness). The reductionists fall into the category of subtle blindness because their non-systemic ways make them blind to even the obvious factors.

Systems way of working is not exactly common sense

This one question I used to face often, "…..if systems are everywhere and everything happens through systems, then the systemic way of thinking must be common sense, isn't it?"

My immediate response is, "Yes, up to some extent this is true, but you know, common sense is not always the common practice."

Common sense is a subjective phrase. What is common sense for you does not seem to make sense to me, and vice versa. This can only be dealt with through the systemic approach. Let's dig a little deeper.

In every process, you'll find obvious things but unless you look through a systemic approach, you cannot tell which one is obvious and which is not. A few months ago, I was handling a complaint about iron casting. When I modelled the system it was very clear that it was because of intermittent pouring. Though the defect was obvious, the manufacturer took it casually. I took some details from them and put them in two columns—obvious errors and substantive errors—to make them understand their process with a systemic approach. Over the next week, I worked with the manufacturer and filled numbers into those boxes. As always, the final summation validated my hypothesis. About 80% of the defects were obvious defects, 78% to be more precise. With just one A3 sheet to look at, I was sure that they would never make or ignore these obvious errors. This was common sense but that too required a systemic approach. Without it, you cannot differentiate between the obvious and the substantive.

Engineers are a little weak in systems thinking

I am an engineer by qualification, a systems practitioner by profession and an educator by interest and desire. As engineers, academically, we are taught in binary systems (e.g. zero-and-one, yes or no) or in attributes (ok or not-ok, go or no-go). This binary system is like a closed loop of education, it limits our thinking to short answers even for complex problems. In the next chapter, you'll learn that 'not going into detail' is one of the barriers to organizational learning. This barrier has a strong linkage with answers being limited to that commonly taught in engineering.

In contrast to engineers, liberal studies students are much better at thinking about the laws of continuity. The world is a continuum and so is the system. Remember, the 3 fundamental characteristics? All 3 of them point to the system's continuity.

On the other hand, if you are an engineer, you can learn systems modelling better than History or Arts students. Modelling becomes very easy for those who come with a technical and mathematics background but it's not necessary for systems thinking. Have you found math being used anywhere till now? I avoid complexities myself, so I don't make things complex for others either. Systems are simple, let's learn them in simple ways.

Despite its simplicity or complexity, easy for one or difficult for others, through the regular practice of the systemic approach and following the right sequence under a good teacher or a mentor, anyone can become a systems thinker or problem solver.

Why do I recommend an intrinsic system?

- To understand your systems or system structure better
- To analyze your system better, the greater clarity you have, the better the analysis and the more accurate your problem-solving approach will be
- Some problems in the world cannot be solved unless we deeply understand what it is affected by. This is true, especially in the case of problems that are inter-systemic or those that are at the edge of two intrinsic systems. Going through an intrinsic system concept makes it easy for you to solve such problems. Even if we cannot solve problems, at least we should know where the problem lies and under what conditions it is becoming a problem so that we can control system behaviour within the current boundaries. If we are not able to solve it entirely, at least we can prevent its recurrence. For example, in one of my investigations related to an aluminium casting part failure, I found problems with variable atmospheric conditions. If I ask that manufacturer to control the environment, it would seem like a joke. So I mapped the system, identified the intrinsic systems, and explained how environmental conditions are affecting the system and, in turn, product quality. They understood and then we jointly prepared a qualitative standard operating procedure (Q-SOP) and a systemic process monitoring method based on the issues that had arisen earlier. This helped update our understanding and reduced the damage that the environment could create. Though we cannot control environmental conditions, we can hand over the control to intrinsic systems.
- It helps us reduce damage. One of my favourite questions is, "How do you reduce the cost of poor quality (CoPQ)?"

It is one of the most discussed topics in management review meetings across the world. In fact, total cost reduction is discussed, but I will take one part of it here, CoPQ. Often, my attendees reply by solving problems. Then I ask, "What if you cannot solve the problem?" The room becomes silent. Even if I repeat the question, the silence persists.

This is the problem. We don't really know how we can reduce CoPQ. Honestly, you cannot solve all the problems, and even if they are solvable, you shouldn't bother about that at first. As soon as you come to know that something is not right, your first response must be to control the damage. Containment, countermeasure and then prevention or solution.

Look at the way the world handled the COVID-19 pandemic. Does any country know the solution? No. Does anyone still know the problem completely? No. All we know is that there is a virus and it is spreading disease. For many months, no one in the world knew the real symptoms, incubation period, how it spreads, and what medicines to administer upon infection. No one had clarity and every country speculated on their own experience. They were saying that the virus was the problem, but actually, it was not. If you put this pandemic in my four-step problem-solving framework, you'll get better clarity. The disease is a symptom (I mean, symptom of the problem), the pandemic is an extended symptom, and we already know, that the extended symptom is always higher in severity than the initial symptom. The coronavirus is our concern, a constraint or a boundary we should focus on, just to avoid scattering our efforts. How did the virus originate? That was our actual problem. The temporary solution that was adopted everywhere was knowing and preventing its infection and spread. If we want to prevent the spread of that or any other virus, we should know its origin, The cause/solution step is still unclear across the world and speculation and blame are going around.

Every country in the world was focused on controlling the damage. Hence, they called for a lockdown. Nobody had ever heard or imagined something like this would happen but it did. We passed the days indoors only so that we could help control the damage. You may not know the solution or it may take some time (like COVID-19). But once the scientists learned it was because of a virus, they came up with a solution (not a permanent solution though). They needed to develop vaccines, but it took time. They didn't know the genetics of the virus. At the same time, since you cannot keep people at risk until you learn about the virus and develop vaccines, the government asked the people to lock themselves till they worked on it. You can reduce costs by controlling damage.

You will also notice that though the lockdown was announced, it was not uniform across the world. The whole system was not locked and some essential services were permitted to function. The government with the help of scientists and doctors identified intrinsic systems and high-risk areas so that they could reduce the damage and at the same time not risk shutting down the entire system.

This is how you can get the benefits of the intrinsic systems. Letting go of the entire system would have risked everyone and locking everything would have hurt people due to a lack of essential goods. Hence, identifying low-risk areas and letting them function under regulatory controls reduced the damage and at the same time helped people live their lives, at least inside their homes.

Chapter 6

Organizational Learning

The words are organization and learning. I have already given you some details about organizations in chapter 2, so I will just be brief here. An organization is a workplace where work gets done at systemic depth and breadth. In organizations, systems do all the work and people act only as influencers.

Learning is the cognitive process of acquiring knowledge. Training, on the other hand, is the process of acquiring skills. Learning and training are fundamentally two different ways of acquiring knowledge. While learning, we educate ourselves from our activities, at our own pace, in our own way, by gathering information from our previous activities or experiments. On the whole, learning is what we teach ourselves. There may be external influencers to help us learn but it is a completely internal process. During training, someone else is designated to provide us with skills. It is the process of acquiring skills from information through one-time influencers.

Organizational learning and learning organizations are not exactly the same. The latter is the product of the former. Organizational learning is the practice that companies need to implement to become a learning organization.

In addition to the difference between an organization, a company or a business mentioned in chapter 2, an organization works with complete systemic depth and breadth. It educates its people through learning and not by training. To understand this better, let us delve deeper into the two types of intelligence.

Intelligence

I work on three types of intelligence—generative, constructive, and regenerative. In this book, I will focus on the first two as regenerative intelligence involves several scientific terms that are not part of this introductory edition.

Some of you might have given psychometric tests as part of your educational assessments or for employment pre-assessments. In the last one and a half decades, since the advent of the usage of algorithmic screening, these psychometric tests have grown by leaps and bounds. If you aspire to join any high-profile job today, be it in a private organization or the government, you will need to undergo a psychometric evaluation. I studied this subject as part of my research work in organizational learning and systems psychology.

Psychometric tests do help employers assess potential employees' non-technical skills such as mental abilities, personality traits, and other characteristics. These tests are designed to assess cognitive abilities, such as problem-solving, reasoning, and memory, as well as emotional and behavioural traits, such as motivation, leadership skills, and interpersonal communication. These tests may include a variety of questions such as multiple-choice, true/false or open-ended questions. They may also include timed sections, which can add an element of pressure and stress to the test experience. Overall, the purpose here is to assess your cognitive capabilities.

I came to know about these psychometric tests while I was in graduate school for the first time and to satisfy my curiosity, I collected some of the questions and started studying them. My purpose was not to pass the test but to understand the concept behind it. In the years since my first encounter with this, I understood a stark reality of the human mind or cognitive capability. Though some researchers have already worked on this and proved that psychometric tests are valid scientific tools, I want to clarify that it has some traps. One of these is the difference between the age of our mind and the age of our body. These two may not match, the higher the age of the mind, the better the cognitive skills. Researchers have also proved this (the method to calculate IQ scores has changed because of this).

How are the age of the mind[5] and intelligence related? In my research, I was able to discern how the intelligence of the intelligent is different from others and how you can tap into it. Yes, anyone can become intelligent because it requires you to diligently follow certain practices. My research is not exhaustive but it is enough to understand the concepts and commence your journey towards becoming intelligent.

Two types of intelligence

Let's delve into your childhood. For my studies, I divided childhood into two parts—one year to 6 years, and 6 years to 15 years. First, I want you to go back to your earlier days, as a crawling baby. Try to recall and remember those sweet old days and if possible prepare a write-up on how you used to learn things in those days (you can observe other kids, of course, many of us don't remember those days because of infantile amnesia. We can forget the memories but not the lessons we learned). When you were a baby, as soon as you learned to crawl, there was nothing in the world that could stop you. If someone stopped you from moving forward, you would most likely scream loudly and angrily.

When a baby goes toward a candle, a mother would normally go and pick it up to avoid any burning, but one philosopher says, "Don't stop the baby from crawling to a candle. Let him learn his lesson."

I observed how babies touch things for the very first time. They never grab anything in a hurry if it is their first instance. They slowly approach and carefully touch the item. But, if you stop the baby from touching it, then it grabs the object. If you don't let

5 Note: I have used the term 'age of the mind' here, in technical terms it can be linked to 'cognitive capabilities increase as we get older' as we develop more connections. I use this term just to make my point that our physical age is not always in synchronization with our cognitive capabilities. If you take graduates from the same school, the same class, and of the same age and give them a set of cognitive capability test questionnaires like a psychometric test, you cannot expect everyone to give the same answers, though they have all studied the same subjects under the same professors. The chances are high that the answers will be different because the age of their minds and their intelligence is different. Why is this? That is the subject of this section.

babies touch the candle, the next day the baby will try to grab fire and the damage will be much worse.

My point here is that children always learn things in generative ways. They approach things slowly and touch them carefully. They learn to stand up by holding something as support. They learn to walk by taking little steps and in random patterns. Children's brains generate or create mental models or mental maps. It is their own way of understanding the world. As a child of two or three years, I don't think you ever believed anything without testing your assumptions. No baby ever does this. You don't know about your country's constitution or the laws of the land. Everything you learn by experimenting and testing assumptions. This skill is the building block of a unique capability, which I call generative intelligence. If you tell a child to not do something, instead of asking you for the reason, he/she goes ahead and does it to see what happens. He/she doesn't ask you the reason for your refusal because he wants to learn the reason by experimenting and testing the assumptions. Sometimes, children break a lot of superficial beliefs through their experiments. If you really don't want your kid to do something, then don't ever tell him that as it will result in the opposite effect.

Generative intelligence is a slow process

Whenever you want to learn anything new, right from the fundamentals, it takes time because, like a child, you need to learn to crawl, stand up, approach easily, and touch carefully to avoid any unforeseen damage. Every researcher and research organization in the world knows that research is a painstakingly slow process. Sometimes researchers themselves get bored of their slow approach, but they know that they can't fly before learning to stand. This is the process of generative intelligence.

The trap of constructive intelligence

Once you reach around 7 years of age, you are comfortable, understand the basics of this world, and can walk and run. Now, you have stopped watching your legs while you walk i.e. just like babies who learn to walk for the first time who are amazed at their ability to walk.

You may have stopped crawling but you have started asking questions, "Why do animals have four legs?"

Your parents and grandparents think that it's better to send you to school rather than answer your never-ending flow of questions. But, unfortunately, they can't escape your claws at night. They have to tell you stories. These stories are building blocks that refine our generative intelligence and make us ready to face the world. The next morning when you go to school, you don't have the freedom to ask questions as you did at home. For a child, schools are like an area without freedom in an independent country. This is the first time you start accepting things without doing experiments and testing. You learn to forget your questioning skills and start accepting whatever you hear. These are the days when you develop formative intelligence or constructive intelligence. You develop your understanding and construct lessons around popular beliefs. By the age of fifteen, you become completely different—from an experimenting child to a completely formed student.

Our education system is designed in such a way that it can help you smoothly transfer from generative to constructive intelligence. Most often you never register this transformation and this is how our world creates crowd followers.

But, there are a few people here and there who never grow up. They are like three-year-old kids even in their sixties. They never believe what you say, no matter who you are. Your academic credentials don't impress them and they don't care about your position and grade. They want to test their assumptions and experiment with things before they ever begin to accept them. We call them researchers, scientists, or sometimes mad people. In my studies, I have found an interesting difference between these people. They never grow out of their generative intelligence phase and do not accept this welcoming and beautiful world of constructive intelligence, where their friends are living comfortably. Instead, they build their isolated world of experiments, test their hypotheses, and find happiness in their slow-moving world, because they generate things based on which others construct their intelligence. All these researchers and scientists are learning influencers.

As part of my research, I studied the life of over 40 achievers and my interesting findings were that people who achieved extraordinary success had few things in common—they had very few friends and had dealt with trauma in life which made them locked into their inner selves. They had begun living isolated lives and had renounced fear early in their life journey. They always believed in change, and most importantly, all of them retained their generative intelligence. I didn't find any good reasons to credit their success to their educational background. They were hardworking but that was not the main reason for their success. Statistics say only a fraction of hardworking people achieve significant success but we cannot credit that success to their hard work alone but also to some internal factors i.e. the characteristics I have listed above.

Generative intelligence correlates very closely with systems thinking. I am working on developing a curriculum to teach systems thinking to high-school children (12-18 years of age). It can be grasped easily at that age and will also aid in avoiding the transition from generative to constructive intelligence which needs to be stopped.

Machines can never have generative intelligence

To explain this better, I will use today's trending example, ChatGPT. My work is not related to ChatGPT in any way but I am using it just as an example here. I have been studying AI and Machine Learning (ML) for the last 3 years and what I found is groundbreaking.

ChatGPT is a Generative Pre-Trained Transformer. The word chat stands for the way the algorithm interacts with you i.e. through chat via a chatbot, unlike a web search.

On November 30, 2022, ChatGPT was released for public use throughout the world. This happened during a very interesting time as I was studying related subjects and this helped me in understanding my research better. I created my account to access this on 15th February 2023.

First, I tried to understand how this platform was created. The developers developed models and trained them using data, the cut-off for which was 2021 (precisely, September

2021). If you ask it anything about current news, it won't be able to tell you. That means that it was trained using available data, collected over the years.

Then, I linked this ChatGPT development with my research—generative and constructive intelligence. In this case, it is not a generative type of intelligence but a constructive one. The designers and developers have trained ChatGPT's algorithms and models to construct responses based on the data generated by human activities.

No machine can have generative intelligence, it is unique to humans alone. All machines can do is learn from our activities and behaviours and construct responses using patterns, structures, or even noise in them, but it cannot be termed generative intelligence.

Why can machines never have generative intelligence? Generative AI is a highly misunderstood concept. If you study all the literature on AI, the developers talk about training their models and algorithms using data, then how can their AI be generative? Is it generating anything? No, it is constructing. Constructing responses based on data it has been trained with. Generative AI is a false idea. Yes, if they teach their models unlearning and relearning, then it can be regenerative but not generative. Artificial intelligence can never be a generative type of intelligence, it is a unique characteristic of natural intelligence.

There are various scientific reasons for this but I will mention only two which are very important. In humans, generative intelligence is powered by the conscious information-processing capability of our brains. Since we have consciousness, we are aware of what we are doing instead of what we are asked to do by someone else (an operator) or something else (an algorithm). No matter the computational speed of computers, they are never conscious. This makes humans unique machines that generate intelligence.

Along with this, our brains have a very complex neural network or interconnectedness that gives us parallel processing ability. This simultaneous processing capability is the cherry on the cake. Though research confirmed that the brain is capable of processing multiple pieces of information simultaneously, cognitive psychologists say that multitasking reduces the brain's performance significantly.

Sophie Leroy, a professor at the University of Minnesota introduced an effect called 'attention residue.' She says that when you switch from task A to task B, your attention doesn't switch immediately. Some residue of task A remains in your thoughts. However, other research shows that with practice and strong awareness of your consciousness, you can reduce this attention residue but cannot completely eliminate it. Whatever it is, consciousness is one of many scientific reasons that give us generative intelligence. These days, multicore processors do have parallel processing, but it is not similar to how our brain processes information.

Thinking and intelligence are not just about processing large amounts of data or making calculations at lightning-fast speeds or processing information at deep sea, it also means consideration of parallel factors like situations, emotions, relationships, consequences, and many others. If you think systems thinking means following a fixed set of practices blindly or following a set of written instructions displayed on the wall, then your understanding of the field is incorrect. That approach is compliance thinking. The main difference between systemic thinking and non-systemic thinking is the cumulative consideration of consequences, the feedback, the intra and interrelationships, and the behaviours of influences and influencers.

A few months ago I got a call from a systems consultant in Chennai. The guy is an experienced programmer with over 20 years of experience in developing computer applications. Six years earlier, he had started a company along with two friends and had developed a platform for quality and document management systems through cloud technology.

In our conversation, he said, "I want to build a platform for systems thinking and design thinking..."

The discussion was a long one. I asked him, "How can a machine think in systems? Systems are highly dynamic, and to think dynamically, you require generative intelligence. But machines can never have this type of intelligence. If you want to think in systems and designs, then work on developing learning influencers and generative intelligence, don't waste your efforts in working on constructive intelligence, they can never think in terms of systems. They will help your thinking but they can never think."

Systems thinking and design thinking are the characteristics of generative intelligence and are not within the reach of machines. Artificially, you can create a brain but not a mind. The mind is the characteristic of consciousness and advanced cognitive psychology says that intelligence originates in the mind, not in the brain[6]. The brain just supports the mind by being a processing unit. Brain—processor, mind—thinker.

What type of intelligence does ChatGPT have?

To further continue my work on generative intelligence I wanted to apply to some universities for academic support. I was writing some research proposals in this regard. While doing that I thought of interviewing ChatGPT to know what it thinks of itself.

My mentor always told me, "If you want insights about someone then go and interview them, information from the media and general public is secondary. First, listen to the man you want to know more about."

I did the same. I conversed with ChatGPT for about two hours and asked various types of questions and it told me what it thinks of itself. One of my questions was, "What type of intelligence does ChatGPT have?"

The reply was an eye-opening call to all the media which is creating hype in the name of ChatGPT, most of the scientific community who are writing series of reports on AI (specifically generative AI) and the ones who are creating these so-called masterclasses to teach how one can take the help of ChatGPT to write emails and do some other stuff!! Go through ChatGPT's answer to my query below.[7]

---

6 Many psychologists and scientists have worked on understanding the relationship and distinction between the brain and the mind. Since it is an introductory edition, instead of giving high level references, I recommend that interested individuals who want to learn some more details on this topic can refer to the article 'Where Do the Thoughts Come From?' by Naresh Kumar, published by The International Journal of Indian Psychology April-June 2021.

7 Note: The text quoted below is an unedited response accessed from my personal account

"ChatGPT is an example of artificial general intelligence (AGI) in the form of a conversational agent. AGI refers to highly autonomous systems that possess the ability to understand and perform a wide range of intellectual tasks that humans are capable of. While ChatGPT is not truly human-level AGI, it has been designed to exhibit some aspects of human-like intelligence.

ChatGPT utilizes deep learning techniques, specifically a variant of the transformer architecture called GPT (Generative Pre-trained Transformer). It has been trained on a vast amount of text data from the internet, enabling it to generate coherent and contextually relevant responses to user queries.

However, it is important to note that ChatGPT's intelligence is primarily based on pattern recognition and statistical associations in the data it was trained on. It lacks genuine understanding or awareness and doesn't possess common sense reasoning or knowledge beyond its training data. It can provide information, engage in conversation, and perform certain tasks, but its responses are limited to the knowledge it has been trained on and may not always be accurate or reliable.

In summary, ChatGPT demonstrates a form of narrow or specialized intelligence focused on language processing and generation, but it does not possess the full range of cognitive abilities associated with human intelligence."

It has given an honest answer about its true nature. It knows that it lacks abilities that are related to consciousness and reasoning beyond the data available on the internet. Under 'how do systems learn their lessons?' in chapter 7 I have discussed a special type of memory called procedural memory. It is a non-declarative type of memory which means we, humans, cannot express them. Still, it is one of the most powerful types of learning abilities that humans have. Such type of non-declarative skills can never be learned by machines because they cannot be converted into data. This is what I wanted to clarify from my interview with this amazing tool—ChatGPT. I will provide my insights from the full interview in my exclusive report on this subject once I complete my work.

Is it true? Is AI going to replace you at work?

Through ChatGPT's response given above you might have understood what AI is capable of. Let me explain this in greater detail using the concepts and findings that I discerned through my research.

This question has two answers. First, no, of course not. But you should also know that AI can replace you if you don't understand how it works.

Developing software powered by AI has become a trend these days when it comes to solving the 21st century's complex problems, but that is the biggest problem. Complex problems require you to think with generative intelligence, with a systemic approach and dynamism.

The difference between complex problems and simple problems is that a simple problem can turn into a complex one when you don't solve it in time or use the wrong method or solve it with a non-systemic approach. In every case, the complexity factor goes on increasing, in other words, complex problems have evolved. No problem turns into a complex one without first being a very simple one. But to identify this simplicity, you must think dynamically, and dynamism is all about generative intelligence. You can never think dynamically with constructive intelligence. To test the meaning of this sentence, go and test any AI model, even the trending ChatGPT. It is not a dynamic tool. AI models are answering your questions, passing difficult exams, and doing so many interesting things but that doesn't mean that they have or are going to have generative intelligence. They are constructing responses based on the datasets they are trained with and as the developers update the data of those models they will also improve but they can never have true generative intelligence and can never become truly dynamic.

On December 11, 2022, OpenAI CEO Sam Altman tweeted, "ChatGPT is incredibly limited but good enough at some things to create a misleading impression of greatness. It's a mistake to be relying on it for anything important right now. It's a preview of progress. We have lots of work to do on robustness and truthfulness."

I thank all those developers for giving this incredible tool to the world but one thing I want to tell them is that no matter how hard they work, and how great a tool they build, it will always be a tool with constructive intelligence, So it is better to change the word generative in the name of their tool to stop misguiding people. It can be regenerative, however, but for that too, it will have to pass certain quality tests. At this level, their tool is just constructive, not even regenerative.

Many AI experts have warned about job losses due to the fast growth of AI tools. They have repeatedly said that the advent of AI would bring job losses unless human employees upgrade their skill sets.

But how do we upgrade? Can anyone answer this scientifically?

The day ChatGPT went public, hundreds of YouTubers came up with their so-called training programmes to teach people how to use the AI tool. Their teaching is like cutting a branch while standing over it. AI tools will never bring job losses unless you allow them to do so and start thinking like them. AI tools are trained using past datasets, so they think in constructive ways. If you start thinking in generative ways, how can they wipe out your importance at workplaces? This is a very basic understanding when you think about job losses due to AI.

As long as you keep learning—not training—no AI tool can ever replace you. Becoming systems thinkers, design thinkers and learning influencers is a solid solution for this existential threat in workplaces. There's a huge difference between natural intelligence and AI.

It is generally said that small companies are training centres of bigger companies. But, in reality, small companies are learning hubs where you'll learn through experimenting i.e. generative intelligence, whereas large companies are training centres. In large companies, they train you to make you an efficient machine, not an effective learner. They train you to follow their compliance culture and constructive intelligence. Most large corporations tell you to think out of the box but don't give you the freedom to experiment. They tell you, "Do what I say, don't be too smart." That's it! Where is the learning? If you have this type of culture, then AI will easily take away your job because machines are superb at following instructions. Just like machines can never acquire generative intelligence, humans can never beat machines in constructive intelligence. In the technological world, both will exist in their places.

Another issue that I studied the last year is the challenge of unemployment. We all know that this is becoming a bigger challenge and is gaining priority in political manifestos and government policies across the world. In my studies, I found that one of the major reasons behind this challenge is not the lack of jobs but the declining employability of employees, especially our students. All companies are searching for the right candidates for their openings. However, the lack of employability is creating a huge gap and forcing employers to adopt machine intelligence or automation. I feel that students must be taken out of this trap of constructive intelligence so that we can teach them systems and improve their employability. In my studies, I interacted with HR personnel and department heads in various states of India and they articulated their concerns. Many of them stated, "Candidates come with degrees and certifications but their employability (ability to work in a workplace) is very poor."

Employability improves when students are taught to transform theories into practical problem-solving. Once again, this does not need the development of certain specific skill sets through training. They can be taught to think conceptually i.e. via systems. If you know systems you'll know everything. Their employability will automatically improve. Generative intelligence is a game changer in every aspect of life because it comes from the systems.

Systems thinking means conceptual thinking. For instance, my systems thinking improved because I met my mentor during my graduation. Every word that I studied in the college classroom was conceptualized by Akash. He taught me how to apply theories in practice. In engineering, we study dozens of subjects and normally, many students pass with just minimal marks without knowing the applicability of the laws and formulae they've studied to solving problems in their workplaces. Systems thinking starts when they start thinking about concepts. While sitting in air-conditioned rooms, engineering students struggle to understand the second law of thermodynamics! This is the bigger reason for declining employability. System modelling became an excellent weapon to solve problems as I can draw concepts, relationships, and feedback through it. I can thus know the inner workings of a system without the ability to go inside it. Some systems are so complex that you can understand them only through modelling such as the extrusion die mentioned in the case study. If you want to solve such complex problems, only systems thinking can help you. This systems thinking comes from generative intelligence. Thus improved generative intelligence or systems thinking is required to improve the employability of students and existing employees.

If you do this, be assured, NO MACHINE CAN TAKE YOUR JOB AWAY.

A brief scientific background about my research on three types of intelligence

In my research, I define generative intelligence as generating or acquiring new mental models through which we understand the world and our surroundings (like acquiring new behaviours, learning patterns, etc.). In the same way, I define constructive intelligence as forming new connections in the existing mental models using generalized knowledge that is available readily (like acquiring specific skill sets).

The scientific difference between generative and constructive intelligence is that, in the former, you initially develop non-generalized mental models and work to generalize them through conceptualization. For example, when scientists study any new field, conduct experiments and research, they work on new ideas that are not readily available. They create the content, establish new relationships, form hypotheses, get them tested, and write notes. These all are non-generalized studies that expect them to generate intelligence. But to make such knowledge a fitting model for general use they need to develop generalized models or concepts (I call them primitive blocks of intelligence) so that others can understand and relate to them. While writing this book, I had to go through my notes over the last 6 years. You cannot understand those notes since they are non-generalized. However, after referring to them, I developed concepts and generalized them.

In the case of constructive intelligence, one develops or forms new connections using already available knowledge or information. It is like constructing intelligence using primitive blocks of intelligence which are the outputs of generative intelligence. This is how AI or ML works. AI machines construct their responses by identifying and relating statistical patterns in the data they are provided. Now you can easily relate this definition with what ChatGPT does. Machines do not generate anything, they construct responses using primitive blocks of intelligence which is available already in the form of data.

I said that generative intelligence is a slower process and let's see why. In earlier days constructing a house used to take years because they had to sculpt stones, prepare gravel and cement-like binder, and cut and carve wood. But now, it is the age of steel structures, precast bricks and ready-mix concrete. Primitive blocks are readily available in the market and all our construction workers do is stack the blocks and cement them. Today our civil engineers can build skyscrapers within the same time as our great grandparents used to build one floor. This is how constructive intelligence works and that is why machines are fast and efficient. Machines cannot be denoted as generative intelligence just by passing IAS or some difficult exams. That is not the scientific definition of generative intelligence.

Let me quote a familiar instance from the movie 'Three Idiots' which can convey what I think about this.

In the movie, the lecturer asks, "What is a machine?"

Rancho tries to explain its definition in ordinary/simple language (or *aasaan bhasha*) or non-generalized words. This is generative intelligence. Whereas Chatur uses the bookish definition or generalized words. This is constructive intelligence. Though everyone expects simple answers (*aasaan bhasha*) they, unfortunately, don't recognize such answers as simple answers are often in non-generalized words. The same thing happened with Rancho as well and the lecturer asked him to leave the class. In the movie, it is shown that ten years later Rancho (or Phunsukh Wangdu) becomes a scientist and Chatur has been chasing him for an appointment.

These new-age machines (with AI and ML) are superb at identifying patterns in the data and restructuring them as per the user's query. If you feed them all the National Council of Educational Research and Training (NCERT) books and provide access to huge amounts of data over the internet and then ask questions, they can easily answer the queries and pass the exams. No human can beat machines in constructive intelligence. They are extremely fast, accurate and precise at analyzing the data. But they fail in many aspects where true generative intelligence is essential like systems thinking.

For example, consider that I feed my book's manuscript into Grammarly, an AI-powered typing assistant. It can restructure my words in various ways, detect errors, give suggestions to rephrase to improve clarity and do many things. But that doesn't mean it is creative or generative. It is generating nothing. I generated the content and it is just constructing my words in various ways. I provided primitive blocks of intelligence upon which AI is building its responses. This is what happens with AI.

To bring the contrast to light, let me state the definition of generative AI given by AI experts.[8] "Generative AI is a type of AI that can create new content (text, code, images, video) using patterns it has learned by training on extensive (public) data with machine learning (ML) techniques." Here the experts are talking about content creation by using publicly available data, it is contradictory to the technical meaning of the word creation or generation. Creation is about 'bringing something into existence.' Since here the data or content already exists, we cannot call it creation. Rather, it is construction i.e. combining things to give it a shape. This is similar to what I explained earlier in technical language i.e. constructing intelligence using readily available primitive blocks of intelligence. Feed the AI machine a huge data bank of human faces (maybe some animal faces as well) and ask it to prepare a new one by providing specific characteristics you require such as the shape of the face and nose, smile, hairstyle, etc. It just identifies the patterns in the faces and constructs another. You cannot call it creation or generation.

From the day I began working on the three types of intelligence, I focused on two areas that needed more attention. First, solving complex problems and second, the field of law.

In the previous chapters, I discussed solving complex problems in much detail. Problems turn into complex ones when we don't solve them in time or answer them using the wrong methods (non-systemic approach). To resolve complex problems, you must think in systems and this is a highly dynamic activity. Hence, it needs generative intelligence. The same goes for law. You need to be highly dynamic in handling cases because humans are dynamic and only then will you be able to solve cases.

Apart from these, another interesting area that I have considered and listed under generative intelligence is creative selfishness or creative dishonesty. The propensity of humans to cheat is also a genius act exhibiting dynamism. I am still working on identifying its scientific nature. However, some researchers have already worked on this. For example, Francesca Gino and Dan Ariely published their work entitled, "The Dark Side of Creativity: Original Thinkers Can Be More Dishonest." However, I am yet to work on this to find out how this relates to generative intelligence.

Just a few days ago, while discussing the progress of my research with my mentor, he said, "Shiva, study animal (non-human) intelligence, you'll get some more ideas."

8 Technology's generational moment with generative AI: A CIO and CTO guide by McKinsey Digital July 2023

However, I had already studied this in psychology. He briefly explained to me how classical conditioning was discovered by Ivan Pavlov, the 1904 Nobel laureate. Though I haven't started my studies on this yet, it is another area I am thinking of i.e. to study natural intelligence (the true generative intelligence). Overall, artificial intelligence can never be generative intelligence. Generative AI is an unscientific and misleading terminology.

I have an exercise for you. After referring to the above definitions and explanations answer this question, "Is a *jugaad* solution generative intelligence or constructive intelligence?"

Role of educational institutions in organizational learning

To solve problems you need three essential resources, i.e. people, money, and time. We get an education in schools and colleges where we have time and people but lack money. By people, I mean not just breathing machines but learning minds. On the other hand, the companies or organizations where we work have money but lack time (everyone expects quick solutions) and learning minds (because companies push employees to a training culture to make them efficient machines). This is the gap we have created by keeping them at both ends. Now, we have to bridge this gap. By doing so, we can build learning culture and learning organizations and even improve employability as I had discussed previously.

I got an opportunity to learn systems through conceptualization by my mentor Akash during my graduation. However, this opportunity is not available to everyone. Most engineers are weak in conceptualization because nobody has taught them in a way they can understand. In cognitive psychology, we study learning patterns. Everyone has different learning patterns, the way I learn doesn't need to be the way you do. We cannot make learning patterns generalized (we should not attempt to do so) and that's the secret of our generative intelligence. At the same time, we cannot live with non-generalized learning. It is a disease as we have seen in the second chapter. We can solve this challenge through conceptualization, something that I have explained in the previous section. Through conceptualization, you can generalize non-generalized content and make it understandable.

Let me take the earlier example of the blind men and the elephant to explain this. We have seen that each blind man interpreted the elephant in his own way. Now, if I ask 10 people (not blind) to study the elephant and prepare notes, there's no guarantee that I will get similar answers from all of them. Everyone looks at the objects in their own way—the way they have learned and understood them. These are what I call learning patterns. Another source from where you can learn about this area is the 2017 article published by Jan Vermunt and Vincent Donche entitled, "A learning patterns perspective on student learning in higher education: State of the art and moving forward." However, I will come up with this subject in my work on three types of intelligence.

Along with systems and conceptualization, Akash used to explain the solutions to real-world problems. This is another problem students face while studying. In schools and colleges, students study hypothetical problems which builds constructive intelligence. On the other hand, if we give them real-world problems they can think more creatively. Though they may not be able to solve such problems completely, the attempt itself teaches them how to approach or look at problems.

The very same idea is applied by some professional education institutes that made internships mandatory. They take students for industrial visits and some form tie-ups with companies and other such activities. However, this is not completely effective due to a lack of systems thinking. We should do all these activities considering systems. Remember, problems can only be at the system level. Hence, if you want solutions you should understand them.

If you can establish this systems learning relationship between educational institutions and companies, you will benefit from generative intelligence to solve problems as learning minds in colleges get opportunities to work on real problems, and companies can take advantage of the students' time by providing them with access.

In the second phase of the learning influencer programme I am working on (I have described the first phase of the programme below), I think that every high school and professional education college should connect with some companies to begin this organizational learning journey. This way institutes and universities can ensure that they are not just certifying graduates but problem solvers and system thinkers. With the help of such graduates, we can easily build a systems thinking community that can solve even the most complex problems with a smile and annihilate this non-systemic culture.

Three dos to get ready for organizational learning

- Stop all training sessions in your company (convert them to learning sessions)
- Stop attending any seminars to learn how to run your business
- Systems psychologists should lead organizational learning

Learning vs. Training

Since my purpose here is organizational learning, I will frequently use examples from that perspective, but they can be simultaneously applied to every field. Almost all organizations use the word 'training' in their employee development plans and intellectual development programmes.

Training is like these motivational seminars, the effect is high but for a very short time. You hire trainers from some external training institutes, they come with their presentation and fancy terminologies like frameworks, strategies, etc. But your people can only understand their words if they have encountered them before, otherwise, they just tune out. As I already mentioned, our mind is a lazy device. It always wants to stay away from mental effort.

On the other hand, you can ask a senior engineer from your own company to demonstrate the work he has done which improved the quality of his line. He will come with a plain presentation, speak in his broken language, and may not have good presentation skills but the effect will be above that seen with the five-star rated trainer. This is because the senior engineer will use language and terminology that is familiar to the employees and will present data from the company with which people work daily. There will be nothing in his broken language which is unfamiliar to the participants. This is what I call learning sessions and this is the very first and significant move towards organizational learning. All training sessions must be stopped and converted into learning sessions.

BRS Behavioral Science defines learning as follows, "Learning is the acquisition of new behavioural patterns." The book mentions, "Methods of learning include simple forms, such as habituation and sensitization, and more complex types, including classical conditioning and operant conditioning."

Take any educational books or go to any school and count the number of times the words learning and training are used. You'll be amazed to find the dominance of word learning over training. For your quick reference, go to any company and count the use of the same words there and you'll be surprised! Nobody uses learning, they talk only about training. If our books and schools talk about learning then where are all these companies and these so-called trainers taking us? This is the reason why despite being an engineer, I am deeply interested in psychology.

How can we convert training sessions into learning sessions?

As described above, your employees learn better when they are exposed to their data. The difference between training and learning is very simple—training is what you learn from others and learning is what you learn from yourself.

Whenever you hire any external trainers or educators, work with them to prepare content to suit the understanding level of your employees and then begin the sessions. Just asking them to give a lecture won't be effective. My request to HR is to not provide training sessions to fulfill compliance requirements. Form an internal education committee, develop training or educational needs based on the departmental inputs and work with educators (internal or external) to build effective content. Most importantly, assess its effectiveness by asking individuals to submit the lessons learned. This assessment works better if you do it without preformatted checklists and ask them to write.

In the Third Eye, I recommend building learning influencers as a solid solution to fulfil organizational learning needs. But as of now, it's a practical problem everywhere that it's impossible to have educators in every business or company. So hiring external educators is necessary but work with them to help you learn better. I have described this in some more detail in a separate section titled 'Principle of Reciprocity' in this chapter.

EYEO—Educate Yourself to Educate Others

It was the first concept I used to teach during the early days of my professional career to encourage people to learn. Self-learning ability is the fourth characteristic of a system (I will write about this later in this chapter) that you can reap only when you develop your talents for yourself.

Some owners used to ask me, "That's okay, we can develop talent, but we don't have such brilliant people. What to do? Where do we find such people?"

Talent is not a special gift nor does anyone have a secret way of developing talented people in high-ranking universities. It is a latent skill that everyone possesses and one which you need to identify, awaken, and foster. Everyone is talented, but that talent is latent for various reasons. The biggest reason is demotivation caused by ego depletion. When you create the right conditions, it will sprout and blossom.

Educate yourself to educate others. By educating yourself, you awaken that latent talent and when it does, you can influence others to learn. This is a very powerful chain reaction. Your every practice becomes organizational learning practice and transforms an ordinary company into an extraordinary learning organization. Learning organizations do not have any special identity nor can you get this title by investing millions or billions of dollars in training and seminars. Put simply, a learning organization is just like any other organization with one key difference—organizational learning practices.

In chapter 2, you learned that business is not about strategy, it is about learning and building your organization's system. No strategy will work if the system of your organization is not in line with those strategies. If your system is aligned with your 6 basic considerations, then you don't need strategies at all. You know that system means confidence, your confidence and that of your customers. Know what your customer needs and structure your business around that need.

Organizational learning and learning organization aren't the same

Be it a company or an organization, its existence depends on the systems it practices and the people working for it. How an organization learns is a very complex subject, but it is easy to grasp if you go through the section on the learning triangle that I have given in this chapter. Sustainable learning in any organization must come from two sources, through systems and the people working for it.

A majority of small companies fear providing learning opportunities to their people. They think that they will learn and join another company for higher salaries, but you'll have that fear if you don't have systems. Neither companies nor organizations have a formal existence, they exist because of the people. If they learn, your company learns and if they grow, your company grows. Provide them with the highest quality of learning opportunities and at the same time use their learning as long as they stay with you for building and strengthening systems. They may go but they won't take your systems with them. Those will remain with your company. Don't ever think that you are teaching or educating your people, think that you are educating your systems through the people. But at the same time, as a leader, you should know how to use their intelligence to improve your systems. It means that you must know how to think in systems.

Organizational learning influences learning in an organization. Like individuals, learning in organizations also happens in two ways—individual learning and team learning. All the aspects of an organization are related via intra and interrelationships. Interrelations are the relationships between an organization and the world, and intra-relations are the relationships within an organization, for example, between functions, between a system and the organizational functions, between people, etc. In my work, I call this intra-relationship intrinsic systems.

No problem in an organization is manifested from individual mistakes. In every problem that I have analyzed and investigated till now, I have always found that the system was in error. An individual commits errors because the system allows him to do so. If the system has only rigidity or resilience, then the possibilities for errors increase. If you approach through a team's shared goal of solving problems you can work out through larger interconnections easily (it is better understood with the learning triangle). The team's shared vision becomes the organization's vision and the team's learning becomes the organization's learning. Though one intelligent person can begin organizational learning, you can only say that an organization is learning when the team develops a commitment to learn and solve problems together. We are living in an interconnected world and working in interconnected organizations, our learning must also be similarly interconnected. I have named these committed individuals learning influencers. They influence others to learn and thereby influence organizations to learn.

Your company or your organization learns through you, it speaks through your tongue, walks through your legs and does work through your hands. What you do directly affects the company or organization. The reputation of the organization you are working for depends on you. Here I refer to not just the individual but also the system.

The learning influencers that I just mentioned are the most important people in my organizational learning research and we will delve a little deeper into them.

How do learning influencers influence?

The first law of learning states that learning is the only process wherein even the worst input can be transformed into an excellent output. The second law states that the greatest learning comes from generative intelligence; learning from your experiments and testing them.

Learning influencers are those individuals who stay ahead in learning, I mean those who influence and help others to learn. They are like catalysts and work to accelerate learning.

In my work, I have given a very special position to this subject. I could easily fill a book twice this size with my detailed information on this subject, but to keep it simple, I will focus only on the aspects that result in solving problems through the systemic approach.

On 13th November 2009 in Leeuwarden, Netherlands, Domino Day was celebrated. Along with Robin Paul Weijers (also known as Mr. Domino) of Weijers Domino Productions, other parties teamed up to set a new world record with the theme, The World in Domino - The Show with the Flow. They lined up a total of 4.8 million dominoes and the first stone was toppled by Jeroen de Meij and the single domino set in motion toppled 4,491,863 dominoes.

The lesson from domino fall is very simple, even a small beginning is enough to influence the biggest change. For every finish, there has to be a beginning. Learning influencers are those individuals who begin the organization's learning.

Building learning organizations means creating a culture of experimental learning i.e. letting your people learn through their work. Until you create a culture where your people have the freedom to fail and still get support to try again, you cannot build a learning organization. Even in the 21st century, this learning organization is just a fictional concept. There is a lot of talk but very little understanding and rarely efforts are made to build one.

Organizational learning is not a new concept. I am not the first author or researcher who is working on this concept but one mind-boggling observation from my studies is that organizational learning has to be coordinated by a psychologist! Yes, you read it right! It has to be conducted by a psychologist i.e. a system psychologist or a learning influencer.

Learning influencers are simplifiers

The world remembers inventors but rewards innovators, that's the reason why Boeing became a large aircraft manufacturer and we see the Wright Brothers only in books. The Wright Brothers invented the aircraft, they proved powered flight is possible, but what did they get in return? They are remembered for their invention but not rewarded. You are a brilliant inventor and have invented a lot of tools and techniques but unless you solve complexities and simplify your creation for the general public you will remain like the Wright brothers. People will remember you but they will reward only those who make things simple, who make it easy for common people to understand and use, who pull inventions out of the laboratories and put them on the market shelves. If you keep teaching 100 strategies and confusing people, they will respect you for your knowledge but never use them. Do not bring in complexities. Work for a few more hours to make it simple and teach only one thing due to which the application becomes easier. Make things understandable for others, and above all, teach yourself first. Educate yourself before you educate others and educate yourself only to educate others. Remember the fifth habit of Stephen Covey's seven habits? It says seek first to understand, then to be understood.

Before we teach others we should learn it from all angles so that we can teach in various ways to make others understand. Whenever it comes to teaching others, I always recall how Swami Vivekananda taught Vedanta to an eight-year-old school-going kid.

Swamiji told him, "Vedanta is like a football game. As long as the ball is inside the court it will be kicked but once the ball comes out of the lines nobody kicks it, it is lifted respectfully and passed inside. This is all that Vedanta teaches us. Until you are trapped in the world, you'll be kicked by your situations and problems but once you come out of those worldly material activities and focus your attention on the Supreme you'll be honoured."

One more Sanyasi who draws my attention when it comes to simplicity is Ramana Maharshi. He taught meditation to a 6 year-old child through eating. Maharshi told the child to focus on his finger while eating. He could keep eating as long as his finger was raised. Once he lowers his finger, he instructs the kid to stop eating. Kids like eating delicious foods and they relish eating. Ramana Maharshi told the kid that this focus is what meditation is all about. You don't have to disentangle from this world to practice meditation or any spiritual activities. You can remain in the world but should not be polluted by it. This is just like lotus flowers, which grow in muddy water. When you pick one, you can kiss it and offer it to the Lord as it maintains its purity even in muddy water.

This type of teaching skill comes when we internalize our learnings and make them easier for others. Swamiji didn't write 100 strategies to learn Vedanta, nor did Ramana Maharshi ever hold 4-hour masterclasses to teach meditation. They simplified even the most complex subjects and made us understand them clearly. This is what learning influencers are about. They are the people who make things simple. The world is simple for those who see simplicity in everything and difficult for those who meditate on complexities. Do not get polluted by complexities, come to the world of the systemic way of learning and working and you will see the magic. Everything will get simplified by itself. Until now, I said, the system has three characteristics—self-maintaining, self-sustaining, and self-balancing. There's one more characteristic that I'm going to add i.e. self-learning. Unless you build simplicity into your system's structure it cannot have this fourth characteristic. Remember, we tend to avoid mental effort.

Learning influencers help you to lift off

On 17th March 2012, just 5 days after my 22nd birthday, I got an opportunity to meet the former president of India Dr. A. P. J. Abdul Kalam (for me he is a learning influencer). It was my first meeting with him. I did meet him after that on two other occasions but the first made more impact on my life. Since 2011, every year during my birthday week, I have made some life decisions that have made a great difference for me. On the same day after meeting with Dr. Kalam, I made a decision that for the first 10 years of my career, I will not bother about how much money I earn, what position I get, or which company I work for, I will only focus on my learning. I knew that if I focused on my learning for 10 years, my journey will lift off. I graduated in 2014 and started my career in 2015. I made my decision about this book in 2023. I vowed this year that I had learned the first 10 years, I will work the next 10 years and will teach for the rest of my life. I am about to finish my learning decade so this book is my preparation for the next decade i.e. the one spent working.

If training prepares you for your work, learning prepares you for life. If training gives you skills, learning gives you wisdom. If training helps you answer questions put forth by others, learning enables you to ask questions for yourself and find answers for them. If training makes you a better professional, learning makes you an influencer. With your train of thought, you can influence others to learn. With your extraordinary problem-solving skills, you can influence others to learn and solve problems. This is why I made creating learning influencers my sole priority.

Only learning can take you on an uplifting journey. I don't believe in any preventive actions without improving systemic practices. There's no prevention unless you understand and strengthen your systemic gaps. This is what I call 'lift-off.' A steep 90-degree approach to your success.

Ability to take correct decisions with repeatability

In the chapter on problem solving, I was asked a question, "If I want to learn only one skill, which one would you recommend?"

My answer was, "Become a problem solver."

Now, if you have some extra time and want to learn one more skill, I recommend that you learn decision-making ability.

Almost all the companies I have worked with face challenges with the decision-making abilities of their managers. They solve problems but hold themselves back from making decisions because of their lack of confidence in their understanding. This confidence factor largely depends on the system you are working with. But there's another area from which it gets inputs and that is your problem-solving skills or the lessons that you have learned in solving those problems. Because of poor decision-making abilities, these decision-makers forcefully influence the system and lead to suffering.

I use an interesting method to improve the decision-making ability of people. I call this method a confidence index analysis. I use this analysis to improve the decision-making ability of the frontline workers and some managers as well.

Whenever we make decisions we need to refer to data. If you are making decisions without data, then you are overestimating the certainty, which I refer to as overconfidence. Don't overestimate as it is dangerous. At the same time, you must take enough care to ensure that the data you are using for making decisions is correct and reliable. Being a manager, whatever actions and decisions you take for improvement are largely dependent on the measurement data provided by your frontline people. Unless you know the accuracy of the data they provide, your actions and decisions have no relevance and sometimes even backfire.

I teach a simple 3-point technique. The data you get has to pass three tests: Accessibility, Reliability, and Usability. The data has to be accessible so that you don't spend precious time editing and filtering data. It has to be reliable as unreliable data makes you less confident. You cannot make critical decisions with such results. At last, the data has to be usable. Reliability and usability are close cousins, confidence is the only factor differentiating the two. Teach this 3-point technique to your team members whenever you expect data from them. First, educate your team members so that you'll have confidence in the numbers they give you. You can never become a good decision-maker with inefficient practices.

The method I use for confidence index analysis is via a standard Measurement System Analysis (MSA) template. I add another column to it and ask the MSA coordinator to get a confidence index from the appraisers. This index ranges from 0 to 1, with two decimal places. When you do this, you'll learn how confident your people are in their measurements and at a broader level, in their work. I started using this confidence index analysis in 2021 and initially, I never calculated the overall confidence index. I just asked the guys to record and give them to me. You know, just this extra number improved their measurement performance by almost double (92%). It means when you ask someone about how confident they are about their decisions, even if you do not register their response (you listen but do not record), it is sufficient to improve their decision-making abilities. Amazing, isn't it?

If you want to improve your confidence, know what you are doing and write or at least understand the lessons from your activities. You solved a problem but did not introspect on the lessons you had learnt. It reflects your lack of seriousness about your problem-solving methodology. If you have solved problems but have not learned anything from them, that is not true. Every problem carries a new lesson. Even if the problem is repeated over 100 times, it still brings new lessons with it.

It tells you, "See, I am here again, there are other ways for me to show you my power."

Never fear problems. Problem solvers will always face more problems but do not fear, just jump in and handle it effectively. Never lose confidence but keep in mind that when you make decisions, ensure that you are not overestimating the certainty.

The ability to make quick decisions comes when you learn and understand the driving concepts of that field or that particular system. Two things that can improve your ability to make decisions quickly include LTQ (Learn Things Quickly) so that you can learn more and SPS (Solve Problems Systemically) so that you are always in alignment with the system of your company or organization. Never ignore the system's signals just to make decisions quickly, remember "wrong decisions also poison the systems." Wrong decisions lead to forced influences and deviating systemic practices which poison the system.

Learning triangle

Do you believe that one person can change the world or at least an organization?

I say, "It depends on who that person is and what he is capable of…!!!"

Let's look at a learning triangle and how learning initiates a growth loop. We have already seen the two laws of learning. The third one states learning is the only cycle, despite being a positive feedback loop or growth cycle, that will never turn into a vicious cycle. Learning is always a virtuous cycle, a win-win for both—the student as well as the teacher, the employee and the employer.

Learning will neither crash the system nor stall it. As you learn more, you work more, and by working on real problems and solving real problems you will learn further. You will get more opportunities and you start to feel better which keeps your cognitive capacity high. Your speed of learning increases even further and so does the breadth of your work which leads you to more learning, LTQ. It goes on like a cycle but never turns into a vicious cycle that will crash the system. Normal laws of nature do not apply to learning, it has its own rules. However, only generative learners can tap into those advantages.

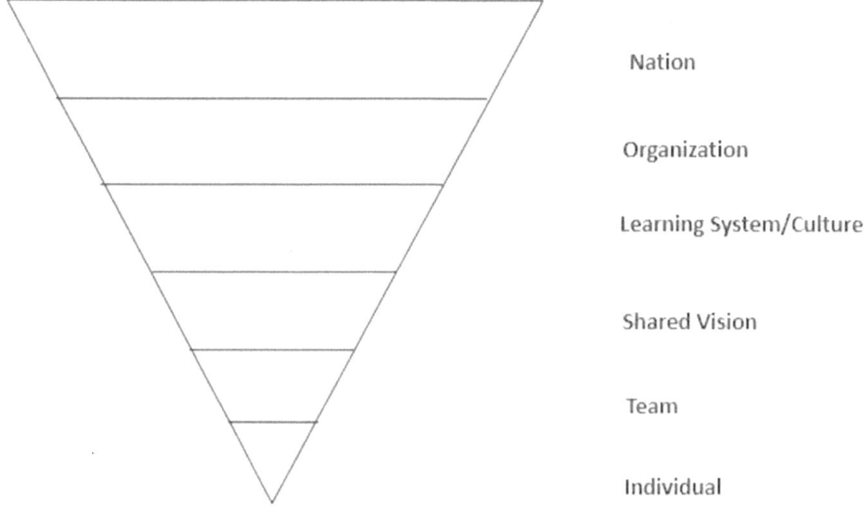

Figure 6.1

An organization or a country doesn't have any formal existence, its existence depends on the existence of their influencers who defend them. Like soldiers defend their country, the influencers defend an organization.

Look at the inverted triangle in the above image. Despite the smaller area at the bottom, individual learning is the most powerful place in the learning triangle. As an individual, whenever you spend time with your books or keep yourself busy solving problems or whenever you learn any new things, not just you but your organization and your country, above all this world is also learning and slowly moving ahead. When you become a learning influencer, you are not just among one in 800 billion people, but you are that rare entity who helps this world learn. This is what I want to show you through this learning triangle.

Individual learning influences teams. They begin learning together and share a common vision for their organization. This shared vision creates an atmosphere, a culture where learning thrives. Though it all started with an individual, now it becomes a community and a culture. This culture initiates a virtuous cycle and transforms an ordinary organization into a learning organization. When organizations learn, the nation learns.

Policy resistance

You need to understand the dynamics of behaviours that cause policy resistance. Everywhere people look at change as threats to their life and/or work. When governments make new policies or amendments to the existing ones, people protest. When a company or an organization hires a new person for a senior position, people play politics. Change management is not an easy concept because of policy resistance.

Why do people resist change? I state two reasons,

- Not aware of the benefits that the changes will bring
- Some wrong hands functioning in the company to resist change

Whenever you bring any changes in your company or organization, make sure you make people aware and show them clearly what that change is going to give them. As long as you talk about your benefits nobody is going to help you in your success. True winning is winning for all, that's why I explained that systems love servant leadership (details given in chapter 4). One way you can do this is through involvement. Stakeholders' involvement is taught in policy design.

Every good systems structure has 6 basic considerations. Two of them are very significant when it comes to managing policy resistance—organizational culture and people skills. The wrong culture fosters weeds in the organizational environment and they spread poison to the culture and the entire system. Sometimes it is easy to identify such venomous people but many times it is really difficult. You might have heard people say that every large-scale illegal business is managed in almost legal ways, with just a thin margin of difference. So they never get caught and sometimes they get support from some strong hands. The same thing happens in organizations too. The people who resist may be your close executives. You cannot see them easily but if you have systems you can have the **third eye** to look for them.

My one-point solution for policy resistance is education—learning. Policy resistance happens because of improving compliance without understanding its essence. If you ask your employees to follow written instructions without telling them anything about the consequences, they will definitely make mistakes in following them. On the other hand, have you ever found children doing any activities without questioning you or without experimenting? No, they don't as they want to learn. Either they question you or conduct experiments, that is generative intelligence. As long as you do not come out of this compliance-based thinking, systems thinking doesn't begin and in the long run, you will face policy resistance.

But, what if organizations with highly sophisticated systems face policy resistance? Just by having systems you cannot escape the trap of policy resistance. Even systemic environments face policy resistance. I haven't completed my studies yet in this regard, but I have tested some of the theories and I will share them. Even systemic environments face policy resistance but to a very minute extent. You can easily deal with such resistance by reviewing the 6 basic considerations. Continuously upgrading your system wipes off most of the resisting forces and when you face problems, dig into them till you reach the fundamental solutions and check what has influenced the system. You will then see the picture. The system is the solution again.

In 2019, I went to Kolkata to work on a problem. After I arrived at the site, I understood that it was not one problem, but a series of them. I did my analysis to rule out some initial considerations, but I started thinking that I was missing something. I worked in isolation for 2 days to understand where to focus. There were no obvious patterns on the surface, but when I drew a system model, the problem was pretty clear. It was the management. One senior executive had used his authority to forcefully influence the supplier. I checked that the supplier did not supply any products directly to the company but supplied base material to others who were the direct suppliers. This was a complex interlinkage.

I contacted the director and submitted my report and asked him to take suitable action, and said, "I can help you strengthen your system but it is your area of influence to take action on senior executives of your company. Such money-motivated hands should not have an influential role in any system." I added some simple checkpoints to their monitoring mechanism and the system was able to keep such things away.

All you need to do is strengthen your system. People become motivated by money because your system has holes, through which they can drain the resources. Just review them and continuously upgrade yourself. How do you remove bugs from your mobile? By upgrading the software, right? Do the same thing with systems. Upgrade the software of your company or organization, by continuously improving systems and no policy resistance can affect you.

I suggested another technique to the Kolkata-based client when the director explained that he could not sack the corrupt executive. You can take action on forceful influencers in two ways, one way is firing or sacking them and the other is using a systemic approach to shackle their hands. Do not fire them if that affects your business negatively. Let them stay but make sure when it comes to negatively influencing anything, the system should fight back. A great system knows how to defend its existence because of its self-sustaining characteristic. I call this technique 'either sack or shackle.' Sometimes, that executive may be a key person in multiple businesses with strong customer contacts (like in the above case). Sacking him would have caused a major disruption, hence adopt the second approach and strengthen the systems to shackle the corrupt hands.

Education and system improvement can solve everything. Every forced influence poisons the system. Unless you think in terms of systems nobody can save you. Think at least ten times before allowing any deviations, before forcing others to deviate from the systemic practices. It's absolutely okay if you don't know but don't influence others to do what should not be done (refer to chapter 4 for the definition of a problem). Some day or other, the poisoned system will strangle you. If you want to build a strong system consider deviations and forced influences as poisons and avoid them. You might have heard that you first make your habits and then habits make you. This applies to systemic culture as well.

Barriers to learning

Some of the most common barriers to learning, both in the case of self-learning and not letting others learn are given below. If your organization has any of these syndromes it's a great setback for your organizational learning.

Not going into detail syndrome

"God gives every bird its food, but He does not throw it into its nest."

–Gilbert Holland

You will not get what you want at your doorstep all the time. Sometimes you have to dig deeper and enter into details. But, how much detail you need to go into is again an act of creativity, intelligence, and situational awareness. Unnecessary digging only uncovers unwanted details. System and design thinking can show you how deep you need to go to learn what you want to learn. In the case study in chapter 4, I went into the details because it was necessary. At every step, after every trial, I did an alignment test and asked myself if that was the problem and if I could stop there. These alignment questions should be asked on your way to finding problems. When you see something related to either system or system structure, you need to stop and do a wrap-up analysis. Of course, digging further will reveal something more but not necessarily. We aim to strengthen our system, that's enough.

Lack of awareness or experience creates this barrier. If people in senior positions suffer from such a syndrome, they become resistant to you and your work. Accepting something as a problem and tagging something else as a solution doesn't solve problems. If you are out to catch a tiger, then catch a tiger, don't catch a cat and paint it to look like a tiger.

Don't want to change syndrome

Some people don't want to change and they don't even let others create change. I have one message for all such people—change is the only constant in this ever-changing world. If you don't believe in change then don't ever attempt to learn anything new, because there will be change in every page you turn to learn.

Gandhiji's famous quote says, "Be the change you want to see in the world."

Such people should not hold any influential role since they can poison the system by avoiding change or forcefully influencing change makers, and resisting policies. Resisting change means resisting policies.

I know everything syndrome

In psychology, this is viewed as an enemy. In one sense it is required i.e. self-awareness is a kind of ego, but a positive one. A teacher has to believe he knows better than his students, this 'better than' is a kind of ego, but it is not a false ego. False ego says that only I know this and nobody else. That is the problem. Ego is required but never think that you know everything, it's simply not possible. There is always something left to be learned.

The definition of ego I mentioned earlier includes a consciousness of your own identity and an inflated feeling of superiority. To understand this, let's talk about a special character, Narcissus. He was a character in Greek mythology who fell in love with his reflection in the water and drowned trying to reach it. That character or the name has become synonymous with excessive self-love—an inflated feeling of one's accomplishments. Highly narcissistic people react with exceptionally high levels of aggression when their ego is threatened or when their inflated self-image is put in danger. The syndrome of 'I know everything' is a characteristic of people with narcissism. Understanding and differentiating between ego and false ego, confidence and overconfidence, and many other instinctive words is very important to improve psychological factors in any organizational setting.

Living on the reputation of one's educational institution

Some people live their entire lives based on the reputation of the institutions they graduated from. Knowledge is not a property of institutional influence. History has seen thousands of personalities who didn't have the privilege to go to school and what they did is being taught at highly reputed universities. Institutes or universities can give you knowledge but not wisdom. That comes from the behaviour you acquire while studying. The moment you puff up, false ego rushes in, and the wisdom comes nowhere near you. Without wisdom whatever you do is just a bread-winning accomplishment, not a world-changing feat. It's good if you are intelligent but don't use that intelligence to show your superiority, just go ahead and solve problems. All the universities were once local. Go back to history and check how many legends graduated from reputed universities. All the institutes earned a reputation after a few ordinary humans achieved extraordinary feats.

Nobody cares about which institute you graduated from, what your IQ is and how many certificates you have in your profile. At the end of the day, what matters is whether you solved problems or just kept messing with them by trading your institution's reputation. People respected across the world are those who are problem solvers. Take any social activist or business icon, they spend all their time solving problems. Many of them didn't even go to school! Understand the difference between privilege and reputation. You may have got the privilege to study in top-notch institutes but don't use that privilege to puff up your reputation. Live life to learn, work, and teach.

HIPPO—Highest Paid Person's Opinion Syndrome

Some companies and organizations have this practice that if a HOD or an executive puts forth his/her opinion, they force everyone to believe it. Most of the time it is good but not always. This creates demotivation and such a mind cannot learn. Learning thrives in a culture where truth is heard and accepted (understand the difference between leadership and dictatorship Table 4.3). Knowledge and wisdom don't come to you by looking at your title or your age, they come to those who put in the effort, who learn things quickly, (implement their lessons and modify their learning based on feedback).

Deviation culture

Every deviation poisons your system. For some specific instances, you can deviate from the standard practice but it gives a wrong message to your juniors and entices them to think that this thing is not so important. Deviations poison the system in subtle and gross ways. The effects of gross poisoning can be seen immediately like online rejections but the effects of subtle poisoning are highly dangerous. You'll never see them in obvious ways but they keep building up in the system till it is too late to do anything. The best example of this is the Chernobyl disaster. The disaster started the day the reactor designers thought of making graphite a moderator, using water as a coolant and making graphite-tipped control rods. A more recent example is the one I have explained earlier i.e. the failure of an aluminium bracket. The failure event started at least a year earlier when the senior employee allowed for deviations. It remained subtle for all those days and exploded when all the dots got connected.

Unless you remove this culture of approving deviations, you can never learn your lesson and become a learning organization. You'll deviate from organizational learning practices too so you cannot learn. Think before you sign any deviations henceforth and do not poison the system.

I am the boss syndrome

> It doesn't make sense to hire smart people and tell them what to do; we hire smart people so they can tell us what to do.
>
> –Steve Jobs

This 'boss' thing is the most damaging agent in any industry. Almost every boss who has become one for the first time has the habit of editing every aspect of their subordinates' work, no matter if it is necessary or not. This creates a sense of disrespect in subordinates but later they start to feel relaxed as they start looking at the boss as a filter of their work. It makes their life easy and the boss's life miserable since he cannot be a filter forever. Getting involved in every mundane activity doesn't make you a boss. You cannot use all the powerful weapons on the first day of the war. You can use your intelligence to decide when you should involve yourself as your organization's reputation depends on your behaviour.

Encouragement is associated with influence and learning, whereas enforcement is associated with creating an impression. Encouragement comes from personal power whereas enforcement comes from the power of position, the 'I am the boss' factor.

Always encourage and influence your subordinates to learn.

Narrow thinking syndrome

I have seen this happening in almost every quality analysis. People follow the easiest option, and you know that our mind is lazy as it hates mental effort. You want someone or something to blame so you define the problem up-front, do some comparative analysis and come up with some nonsensical findings as the cause of the problem. This narrow thinking does not take you anywhere. Think with a wide-angle lens, explore all the possibilities and analyze every possible combination to identify the real problems. This is the same thing that author Mike Rother wrote about in *Toyota Kata* (described in chapter 4).

Another area damaged by this syndrome is management. Some issues are actually the problems of the organization more than the individuals. Since we are talking about organizational learning, what the organization does matters more than what an individual does. Establish rigidity in the organization but at the same time give it resilience. Give people the flexibility to tap into new ideas. Narrow-mindedness is a more common disease in both companies and organizations. Just saying 'think out of the box' doesn't help unless you allow your people to experiment and learn through generative intelligence.

Crunching numbers syndrome

If you are not good at numbers, don't worry! Number crunching without analytical skills is actually a disease. In my systems career, I have worked with some of the most fascinating statisticians. They are more calculators than problem solvers. I always tell my participants to not become mere calculators and try to understand what the numbers are saying. Design thinking helps you immensely in understanding trends that numbers often expose subtly. Unless you develop the skill of listening to the whisper of the numbers, you cannot solve problems without significant damage. In research, common approaches for analysis include quantitative and qualitative ones. Numbers crunchers follow a quantitative approach. They wait for sufficient sample sizes before taking any decision so that they can calculate the mean, standard deviation, etc. This is like waiting for an accident to happen so that a better analysis can be carried out. But sometimes, you have to take countermeasures just with one piece of data. This is where the number crunchers face difficulty, and design thinkers with a qualitative approach have an edge over them.

Brand reputation syndrome

Just like students and professionals live by trading the reputations of their educational institutions, companies and organizations live by trading their past brand image. This is not bad if you are providing quality products, but don't live by your past image.. What you do today and how your system is operating today matters more than what it used to do. Don't live in the past, and keep your system always upgraded so that you'll have a competitive advantage over others. In my 6 basic considerations, I have mentioned environmental considerations in which you'll continuously assess the business environment and this makes your system stronger. What you do today is more important than what you did yesterday and what you'll do tomorrow, so focus on system strength, not the brand image. If you have a system you'll gain a brand image automatically, without any extra effort.. Learn from yesterday and work today to strengthen your system for tomorrow. The system takes care of your brand.

Learning influencer programme

This is a long-term programme under my organizational learning research. When I was about to name the programme I had designed during my organization learning research, I did a deeper psychological study to know when our mind opens to learn something and what precautions need to be taken to ensure continuous learning. All my findings were centred on influencing not creating an impression. With your intelligence, you can impress others. But if you want to teach them something and if you want others to learn something from you, then stop impressing people and start influencing them. Your intelligence is useless unless you use it to solve problems as well as to teach others and to do this you must learn how to influence others so that their cognitive capacity accepts what you teach them. No matter how many facilities you provide, no matter what titles and certificates you hang around your neck and no matter what incentives you provide unless you influence learners, learning cannot happen.

My purpose in this programme is to help professionals and businesses to:

- Design and build systems with four fundamental characteristics and 6 basic considerations
- Solve problems with a systemic approach
- Use psychological understanding as part of the problem-solving method (systems psychology approach)
- Assess the confidence of your team often to make them better decision-makers
- Foster learning in a working environment
- Give people the freedom to fail and still support them for further experiments (generative intelligence)
- Provide systematic steps to create situational awareness

To summarize the concepts and my studies I designed campaigns such as, "**One Organization One Voice Campaign**" or "**One Company One Voice Campaign**" and "**Problem Solving Campaign.**" Let's see each one in some detail.

One Organization One Voice Campaign

If you study successful organizations and failed companies, you will find one common truth. Those who shared their vision won the race and those who didn't rotted in the mud.

Many organizations, despite having systems and working with systemic depth and breadth, lack one essential organizational skill i.e. the power of being focused. They hire multiple consultants from outside and think that two heads are better than one. Yes, this is a good thought, but only when those two or three heads think of the same goal or focus on the same organizational goal.

We designed our systems structure by taking into account 6 basic considerations and in my system's definition (first definition) the third important word is objective. When it comes to a company or an organization, all individualistic interests have to cease and only the system's objectives must be taken forward. More is good, but only when all focus on one objective, i.e. the system's success. If you lack focus, then more is dangerous. We have seen this in the section on systems and strategy and the chocolate experiment.

This campaign helps avoid the efforts scattering effect. In my career, I have often observed that companies and organizations don't focus on important issues. You may be aware of the Eisenhower matrix. It is a 2×2 matrix, popularly known as Action Priority Matrix, Urgent-Important Matrix, Time Management Matrix, and many other names. This matrix talks about urgent tasks and important tasks. If any tasks are becoming urgent and important, it means that you are not planning your time and resources well enough. In project management, it is taught that failing to plan means planning to fail. The tasks that you list in the emergency or urgency category (Do quadrant) are your failures. Even if you complete them successfully, you have still failed because you haven't managed your resources well. Commonly, companies work on urgent activities. Every email and phone call has the word urgent in it and mentions 'the tasks that need to be completed immediately.' If you dig deeper into the cause of this urgency, you realise that they haven't planned their tasks until those activities came and sat on their shoulders. Till then, they were busy with some mundane work, non-priority projects or some other non-value-added work. They spent time scattering efforts here and there and at the end of the project timeline they became trapped in a tight deadline. Arrange the activities in terms of their priority and execute them in that order. The second quadrant, the plan quadrant, is the best to execute work.

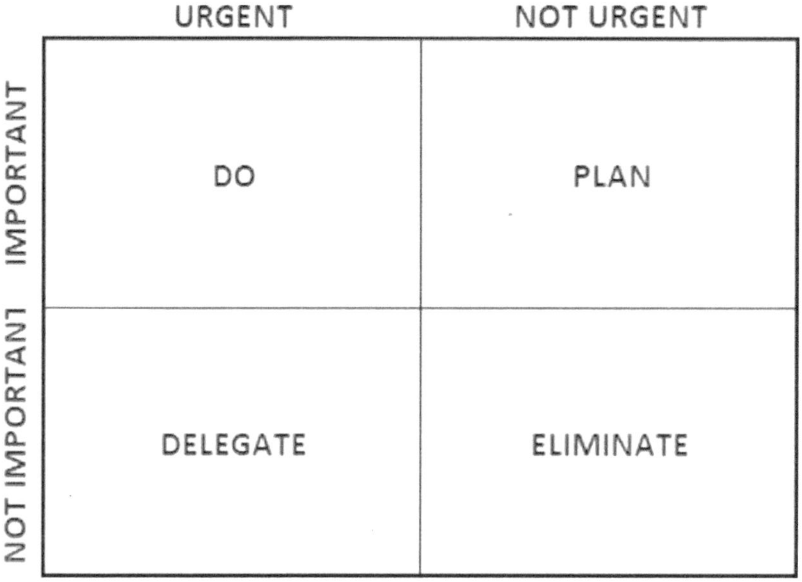

	URGENT	NOT URGENT
IMPORTANT	DO	PLAN
NOT IMPORTANT	DELEGATE	ELIMINATE

Figure 6.2

Use this matrix and plan your activities well in time and follow them accordingly. The lack of effort utilization was my observation while working with multiple clients and in my organizational learning research, this is what essentially made me come up with the One Organization One Voice campaign.

In this programme, you first need to do organization transformation profiling by studying what that organization wants to achieve and the depth and breadth of its system so that existing resources can be assessed. So scattering resources can be curbed and any lack of skills or abilities can be filled by building learning influencers. Along with profiling the organization, it is necessary to profile individuals who, in one or the other way, influence the system. Again, for this, we need to use both the depth and breadth of our skills and learning abilities.

In my studies, I used the Awareness, Interest, Desire, and Action (AIDA) model to create a profile of individuals. I try not to invent any new models and use the models and frameworks that are generally known. AIDA is a widely known concept used by marketers across the world. Through my experience with my suppliers, I can say that just by making people aware of their tasks you can improve effectiveness by as much as 30%.

Awareness is the beginning, **interest** is the next important step. You can develop an interest in them by mentioning how important the quality of their task is and how severe the risk involved is if they committed errors. Ensure that you do not hurt them emotionally. Great education without empathy will drive even the best interests away, so be empathetic in your teaching and mentoring. Though interest is external, **desire** is internal. Interest is similar to enforcement while desire is like encouragement. When you mention the importance of quality and the associated risks and do it without hurting them, you activate a subtle desire in your people. That is enough to activate true human intelligence or generative intelligence. The purpose of all the first three steps is to make one ready to act or take **action**.

Another famous model from Edward Deming is PDCA (Plan, Do, Check, and Act) which comes close to the AIDA model. But for psychometric profiling, I prefer using the latter which is more effective than the former. PDCA talks more about action and less about human interest and motivation (desire) which are psychological factors.

Make people aware, develop an interest in learning, awaken the desire to experiment and learn and then give them opportunities to take action. Let this loop continue. This is a simple organizational learning process. Learning will never happen if the person is unaware of its certainty—what is to be done, how to do it and why. Without awareness, interest does not develop, and without interest, there is no motivation to take action. So, this learning loop does not work in reverse.

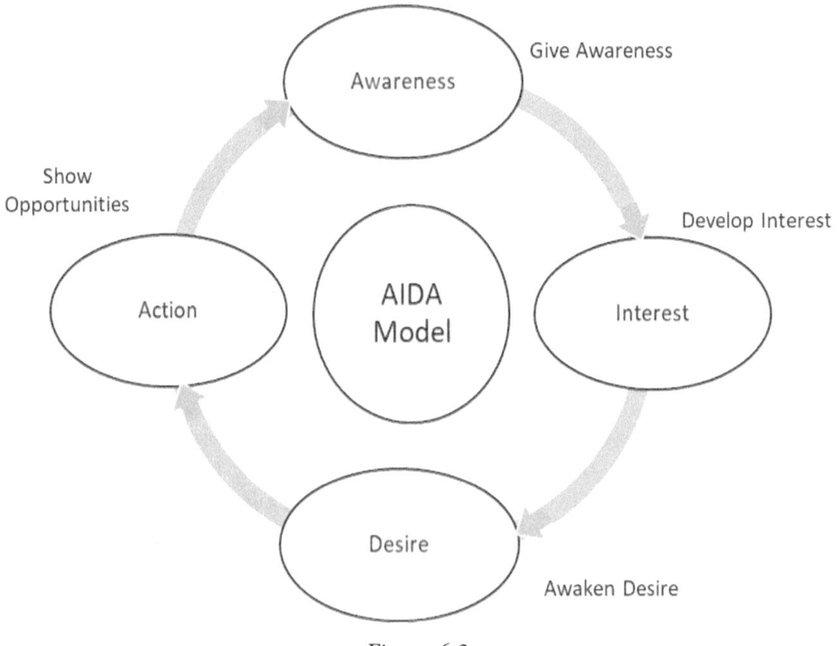

Figure 6.3

Developing an interest means pushing a behaviour continuously. As you keep on pushing, you awaken that person's internal desire. When you do that, you don't need to tell him/her how to do the work. Just tell him/her what you expect (NICE) and he will do it on his own.

You have awakened the desire in him/her, the desire to work. This is active education, not passive. Training is a passive form of teaching, whereas learning is an active form of education.

These days it is a very common practice for HR to work on employee competency mapping. This is a better practice than just writing down job descriptions. But the difference in transformation profiling that I have developed in this **One Organization One Voice Campaign** is that I talk about profiling your company or organization as well along with profiling your people so that you could know as a company where you stand and what you are trying to achieve. The majority of growing companies make this mistake. They try to expand the business by just hiring more marketing guys or investing in R&D. But it is not the right way. Profile your company first and focus your resources on your strengths. Transformation only happens when your organizational profile meets your people profile, unbalancing one essentially unbalances the entire system.

Problem solving campaign

The second programme I designed is the **Problem solving campaign**. This model is actually a one-year campaign and the objective is that 'everyone should solve one problem a day.' Just one problem in line with their job roles and responsibilities. But it had to be solved in a systemic manner, not as a quick-fix solution. If you are efficient in solving problems and have sufficient time after solving yours then go and help others. But ensure that you don't order others. Don't sit on a chair and dictate to others. Be a mentor who neither dictates nor markets himself/herself. Real mentors guide their mentees and are the advocates of the I Do, We Do, You Do model.

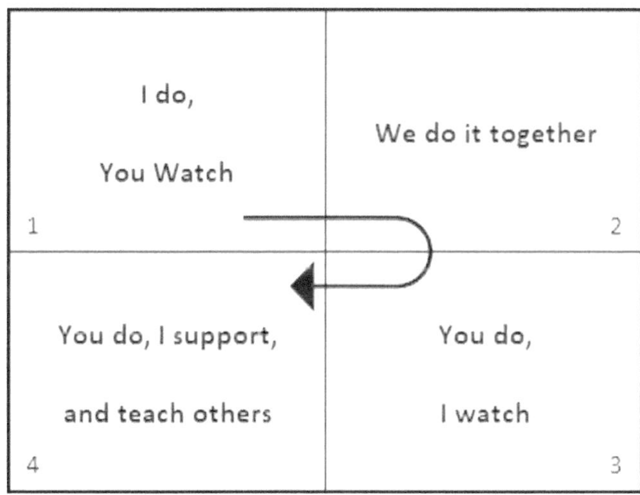

Figure 6.4

For any company or organization, lessons learned from solving any problem are more important than solving problems. You need to ensure that after solving every problem, your team writes down the lessons learned. Every systemic solution has something to teach individuals as well as the organization. At a broader level, it can also teach the world if it is a breakthrough solution. You have to identify those lessons and record them. Once you complete this campaign, the team's next step is to form a problem-solving forum where the solutions will be discussed and horizontally deployed to strengthen the system. If your organizational policy allows it, teach those lessons to others so that you can become an influencer. What did Toyota do when it entered the US market in the 1980s? It taught the Toyota Production System (TPS) to others who showed an interest in learning. What did the Motorola guys do in the 1990s? They invited people to learn the Six Sigma practices. They never labelled it as a proprietary practice or tagged it as their invention, instead, they taught people. Learning and teaching have to go hand in hand without any expectations.

You may reduce the duration of the programme to 6 or even 3 months but I recommend a year so that your team and organization can learn their lessons better since there are a lot of activities in this programme to work on. I know that everyone cannot solve problems with equal levels of severity, so I have defined various tools that you can follow. I have listed 10 tools here. I will not go into the details but you can understand more from my website. In brief, these include

Cut-up technique

- Design thinking practices
- Statistical tools (control charts, run charts, trend charts, process analysis, Six Sigma tools, etc.)
- Analytical tools (fishbone diagram, AIDA model, PDCA model)
- Layered audits
- Advanced Risk Assessment (categorization of failure into latent failure and active failure, qualitative and quantitative approach)
- Identifying problems using observational and process approaches
- System modelling and feedback analysis
- Four-step problem-solving framework
- Swiss cheese model

You can teach people these tools based on their skill levels but ensure that every tool is used to solve problems in systemic ways. The right tools when used in the wrong ways damages more than the wrong tools used in the right ways. So always keep an eye on how your people use tools. The World Wars are a classic example of tools that were developed to defend the country being used to destroy the world.

Along with using these tools, focus your attention on project management, it is becoming very important these days. Some of my suppliers ask me how to use Six Sigma tools and methodologies in simple ways as it is well-known that these projects are very costly. So even large organizations go for alternative ways of solving problems. I always say that if you know something deeply, you can easily find ways to simplify things. Every problem does not demand that you use all your tools. You should learn various tools to solve problems but you needn't inject all your tools into every problem. Some of the high-impact problems can be solved with simple tools.

You might have heard, "If you know only one way to solve a problem, it means that you haven't understood the problem well enough."

Be it Six Sigma methods or project management tools and techniques, if you have learned the subject from someone who simplifies things, you can simplify it and get the same benefits without any additional costs! It is important to know if you have learned or have been trained.

Just to give you an idea, let's say your organization works five days a week with 100 people. Every individual can solve 230 problems a year, considering that he/she works for 46 weeks. The organization can solve 23,000 problems!! An amazing number, isn't it?

Solving 23,000 problems a year is not a small achievement. Along with this, those individuals need to collect lessons learned from their solutions. In just one year, you will have enough data to solve any problem in just 10% of the time in the coming years. This is the concept behind this campaign.

Please note that though I call these concepts campaigns, the underlying purpose is to create awareness and initiate actions. We celebrate safety week, environment day, and earth hour but it doesn't mean that we think about safety during just that week or take care of the fragile environment on that day alone or commit to saving the planet in that one hour, the purpose is to spread awareness and bring new initiatives to improve practices. The same goes here as well, when you think of improving something have a larger picture in your mind so that you don't just see what is obviously visible but also look at something that doesn't show up. This is my purpose behind these campaigns. Always look beyond what you can see and listen beyond what you can hear. If you understand the meaning of this one line then you're a certified systems thinker.

As part of my research on systems psychology, I wanted to initiate a discussion with commercial pilots, since my first systems thinking mentor was an international accident investigator. He used to tell me often about air crashes and that planted a seed in me. He awakened my desire to know more about piloting skills and how pilots handle those huge metallic objects thousands of feet above the ground.

During my earlier studies, I realized how important systemic involvement is in piloting an aeroplane. The aeroplane manufacturers installed FDR (Flight Data Recorder) and CVR (Cockpit Voice Recorder) just to make sure that there's a systemic provision to keep an eye on how the main system (the plane) behaves and how those influencers (the pilots), influence the system. FDR and CVR are like the **third eye** of the influencer but they are beyond their influence. This systemic eye has transformed investigating accidents from speculation to a systemic approach.

I had informal conversations with five pilots and their words of experience helped me in understanding a lot of things such as their training, the importance of situational awareness and presence of mind, and many more. When I asked them what improvements could be made to the system, they were very kind and candid with me.

Three pilots said the same thing in slightly different words, "Our planes have a lot of system monitoring devices like FDR, CVR, and many sophisticated sensors but most of the time this data is used when something happens. If we are trained on the basis of the recorders' data, we can perform even better and keep our planes and people safe in the sky."

In other words, they meant that why should investigators focus on what went wrong in a particular situation instead of looking for something broader? When there is a crash, investigating officers carry out a fantastic investigation, uncover a lot of facts and recommend actions for prevention. But do they ask airlines to keep an eye on how their pilots operate daily like analyzing FDR and CVR data regularly and following some systematic methods? If this is not done, then you are just waiting for the accidents to happen. For a better operation of any system, gathering and analyzing system signals frequently and educating those influencers about possible issues is important so that they know how to respond. Any serious event rarely happens without giving enough prior signals, but if we keep on ignoring them thinking that they are small and assuming that our pilots are well trained to respond appropriately, it might lead to trouble. If you continue to ignore system signals, then it is murder, not an accident.

Instead of training your people using standard tools and some simulated situations, use their data to educate them. The collective experience of the team arranged in a systemic model provides real learning and leads to the development of generative intelligence whereas simulator-based ones are training leading to the development of constructive intelligence.

If you practice these two programmes correctly, it can change any organizational culture to a learning culture and a learning organization is an outcome of organizational learning practices. This is the difference in my research. I call organizational learning a set of practices that can take any ordinary business or company or organization to a learning organization.

When you successfully practice the tools given above and implement the learning influencer program, you'll add the fourth characteristic to your system i.e. self-learning. This makes you ready to launch every day as an innovation day. Your organizational learning practices become your first point of reference and your customers look at you as problem solvers, and your suppliers look at you as proud customers.

Another insight that I received from the pilots was in answer to my question, "What do you do if you sense a storm building ahead? Would you inform ground controllers and wait for their instructions, or you take action on your own?"

I asked 3 pilots this question in order to see if they would try to influence the system in difficult situations. Again their replies were similar. They said, "Of course, we will inform ground controllers, but we take action too and configure the plane for stormy situations to save it. Being pilots, our only priority is to keep our planes safe in the sky. The plane is designed to sustain storms but it all depends on how we handle the systems."

This answer can teach us an important lesson. Every carefully designed system is capable of sustaining itself under tough situations. It is the characteristic of a system. All you need to do is configure your system, and this means, identifying influence points and observing how the system behaves under two influences (internal and external) and two relationships (inter and intra). Understand the behaviours of your systems and put in continuous efforts to strengthen systems to rebuild yourself.

Slingshot effect

Acquiring the fourth characteristic requires dedication, focused effort, and the team's shared vision. Once you do, your organizational growth gets propelled by transformational velocity. In orbital mechanics and aerospace engineering, scientists use the gravitation pull of astronomical objects to direct a spacecraft or to increase its speed. This is also called gravitational slingshot. This slingshot effect saves a lot of fuel and money. Similarly, the self-learning characteristic brings a slingshot effect to your organization and saves a lot of effort in solving problems.

Sustainable improvement for achieving excellence

When it comes to systems implementation through any certification, the first thing you learn is continual improvement. For years, I used the same terminology, but when I began working on organizational learning, I thought that something was missing in these words, something more could be added to make it more meaningful. I am going to introduce another concept now which enhances everything that you have learned so far and adds another feather to the cap of systems learning.

You know a lot about effectiveness and efficiency and continual improvement talks about these in much detail. I am going to take it further to the third E, excellence. I call these the 3Es of systems implementation, Effectiveness, Efficiency, and Excellence.

How do we achieve the third E? I follow a simple method i.e. risk management. In my practice, I study and manage risks at 3 levels—product, process and systems. Do not jump directly to systems-level risk management. Connect continual improvement practices to systemic approach and generative intelligence, thereby learning to achieve sustainable improvement for excellence. While achieving the first 2Es—Effectiveness and Efficiency, you will come across many problems and if you solve all those problems through the systemic approach, learn your lessons and incorporate those in strengthening your system structure, your journey to reach the third E becomes easy. You can say that you have reached it only when you get to the fourth fundamental characteristic of a system i.e. self-learning.

Whenever I decide to improve the systems of any supplier, my first focus is to protect product quality so that I ensure that we are receiving good quality products. This is product-level risk management. Then, I turn my focus onto process-level improvements as the lessons learned through product improvement provide direction for managing process risks. Finally, I turn towards system risks when I have enough data and lessons from both these aspects.

Further, we need to transcend our improvement efforts to achieve sustainability. Sustainability does not mean business continuity plans alone but with all 6 basic considerations. Every good system takes care of other interconnected systems like that of your suppliers and customers. Today's companies and organizations have wider responsibilities towards the environment, society and governance (ESG) along with their growth so that they achieve holistic sustainability, all culminating in excellence. Business continuity can be best achieved with holistic sustainability through the systemic approach.

Improvement for excellence cannot be achieved in a month or even a year. Two things are essential if you want to reach excellence, time and effort. You already know that generative intelligence is a slower process and requires continuous efforts.

Every sustainable improvement should follow the three levels of risk management to make sure that the time taken to improve your system doesn't hurt the customers. You need to ascertain that they believe you and feel confident in your products. Your products give you real data about your process capability, and that gives you a clear picture of the strength of the systems. At the end of the day, excellence comes from building stronger systems but working on the system without knowing the products and process risks can disorient you and blind you to most of the factors. This is one of the reasons for my work on intrinsic systems concept, to look at the systems in detail. Follow product, process and system assessments in sequence, and provide sufficient time and effort.

Principle of reciprocity

You might have heard, "Never hide anything from your doctors and lawyers." In the same way, when it comes to learning, "Never hide anything from your educators."

Whenever you hire any external service providers such as educators, tell them the truth about your objectives, your plans for growth, how you handle your employees, what you think about society, safety, and anything relevant about your business or your company. By doing so, you will help them give you better service. In the end, you will build better systems together.

I have come across many such instances where some executives or owners give basic information or piecemeal inputs like answering in attributes to the questions asked by educators or consultants. If you do that they won't be able to understand your thoughts and cannot give you foolproof or error-free solutions.

Education works on the principle of reciprocity. I already mentioned at the end of chapter 4 that 'knowledge without humbleness is of no use.' The same goes for students as well. Akash used to tell me the characteristics a student must have. Honesty and reciprocity are at the top of the list.

As a student, if you have some dreams and any plans for your career, share them with your teacher, they can help you achieve them. In my primary school, my class teacher Kudabale sir asked me, "What are your dreams? Who do you want to become?" I didn't have any ideas about those questions then. But through his two questions, he set me on the path to finding answers. That's how a real teacher helps a student.

Never underestimate the power of reciprocity. It works even in organizational learning as well as it works in general education. Reciprocate and work mutually with whatever external service providers you hire so that you achieve better education and transcend to a learning organization.

Effect of lack of learning culture on the society

Incompetent managers are responsible for top management thinking of switching to automation, which later leads to layoffs. They hire consultants or buy software to restrain their top executives, essentially risking the workers' positions. I studied over 20 years of literature to know how and why this automation industry took birth and how it is going to affect our lives and destroy the middle-class economy in the long term.

Automating tasks or implementing machines or software may help the company achieve efficiency but it affects the company's dynamism and destroys generative intelligence. This is because though the industry, like the world around, is highly dynamic, machines are highly static in their tasks and can do only what you have programmed them for.

Dynamism can be achieved through a learning culture. Training culture helps you to create breathing machines or trained people, whereas learning culture helps you to create generative intelligence and the most powerful and dynamic machine, the human being. I call such people learning influencers. I am always against the suggestion of reducing manpower in any workplace. I recommend that owners should think about how they can employ more people so that they can feed more stomachs (social objective) but at the same time use their intelligence, provide better learning opportunities, develop and strengthen their systems and grow their ordinary company into an organization, more specifically, a learning organization. A learning organization along with its learning influencers is an asset to this world that contributes to society and the environment. This is a holistic sustainability model.

If you keep a machine idle, you still need to pay for its overheads like insurance and instalments if it is on loan, but for a human employee, even if you don't give him/her any work, he/she will still find something to do and get involved in solving problems. A human can never be a liability unless you don't know how to use his/her generative intelligence. If you achieve this level of learning by following the learning triangle, the entire organization becomes a hub of generative intelligence and systemic thinking. Every great and successful organization has done the same thing.. They achieved holistic sustainability through organizational learning practices and became learning organizations. Another attribute that I would like to add to the concept of organizational learning, is systems psychology.

Chapter 7

Systems Psychology

Ideal place to work

What does an ideal workplace mean? I started working on organizational learning and systems psychology in 2019. For the first year, I studied academic literature and manuals of official standards and then I turned to surveys, interviews, and experiments. I interviewed almost 300 people.

I asked a straightforward question, "What kind of a company do you want to work with?"

Although the answers were varied, when I put them all together in one place, I could see clear patterns. Some of the responses were that an ideal workplace means a profitable company, a company that has employee-friendly policies, a company with great leadership, no layoff history, a multinational group, a listed company and, in a lighter vein, a company that pays more and pays on time. All these are absolutely correct, there was no doubt about it, but I still felt that something was missing. I learned that in the second part of my studies when I started interviewing senior levels like managers and executives.

You learned many things about systems in previous chapters such as 6 basic considerations, various concepts, organizational learning practices and so on. Using all this knowledge, can I say that the ideal place to work is one that has systems? Or one that solves problems and that too in systemic ways or a learning organization that follows organizational learning practices? Can you picture such a place that has all the characteristics that I have derived from my interviews?

If you go on listing all the characteristics that people think about, it will remain a never-ending list. To summarize, can I say that the ideal place to work is a learning organization? But the biggest question is, where can we find such a company and is the supply of learning organizations enough to employ everyone? Well, though the question is obvious, the answer is not very clear or easy.

In the previous chapter, you have studied how an ordinary business or a company becomes a learning organization. It is the people who make that happen. But again, the question remains the same. How? I'm trying to answer this question in my systems psychology research. Since this book is an introductory edition for systems psychology, I will briefly walk you through this amazing study that I have worked on. Some concepts are deeply technical and scientific but I have done my best to simplify them. Still, if you find any difficulty, you will find the answers in my upcoming publication which I have dedicated to this exclusive subject. I added this chapter in this edition because it is necessary to complete the loop for initiating systems thinking and begin your journey towards becoming a learning influencer. I want to provide you with the **third eye**.

Many companies develop systems and work on improving them but once the company becomes an organization, managing systems becomes a heavy task. They don't focus on the system's behaviours and go back to square one. They have systems but deviate from systemic practices. This happens when you try to become a learning organization without strengthening organizational learning practices, and without learning lessons from your work.

If you ask me to distil this entire book into just a few words, I would say, "The Third Eye is all about learning—systems, system structure, systems influencers, situations, behaviours, and organizational learning practices."

In these 6 words, you will find everything that I have written in this book and what I am doing in the real world. To further simplify these 6 words and dozens of concepts and tools, I am working on systems psychology or learning systems behaviours. How systems behave in different situations and how you can learn about systems better so that you can predict their behaviour well in advance. It is just like predictive analytics. Those algorithms analyze patterns in a large pool of datasets and make predictive guesses for the next data point. This is what criminal investigators study, the behaviour of the suspect to predict whether he/she had any means and motives to commit the suspected act.

To put it succinctly, systems psychology means how people interpret the systems of which they are a part or an influencer. How what goes in i.e. the input or the behaviour influences the output.

Systems psychology is made up of two words, systems and psychology. You already know a lot about systems and psychology is a branch of science that studies behaviours—actions that can be observed and measured. Through a deeper understanding, you can learn how to predict those behaviours. Though psychology has many branches, we don't have systems psychology as a branch of study, as we don't study systems as they should be. That's the biggest problem and the main reason why our solutions don't solve problems. We have branches like cognitive psychology in which we study cognitive behaviours and the internal processes of the mind. There is social psychology in which we study people and their relationships with others, with groups and with society as a whole. In other words, the study of social behaviour. We have animal psychology in which we study animal behaviour. Similarly, there is child psychology to assess the development of children and so many other branches of psychology.

But there is no systems psychology since we don't study systems at all. Systems psychology is the study of systems and the relationships between each of its considerations and how the influencers influence a system leading to a particular behaviour. This is done to improve the psychology of a system to achieve better system performance.

We have various statistical tools to predict process behaviour so that we can take action before things go out of control. There are tools like histograms, run charts, control charts, and many others that help us make objective predictions by analyzing patterns and trends in the data. But what about systems behaviour? How can you know what your people do and say? You cannot keep asking everyone and in reality, a lot of errors are being committed unknowingly or through situational pressures. There are no tools to study systems behaviours and there is no field of study or department for research. In quality, we study foolproofing or error-proofing the processes so that the human error factors can be minimized, if not eliminated. We don't have such a thing in the system. Can't we implement a system that is foolproof or error-proof? Unless you error-proof your systems, all your other solutions will be similar to providing a license to manufacture cigarettes and putting in regulations against its sales or placing the warning 'smoking is injurious to health' or 'smoking kills' on packets. Obviously, a worthless attempt.

Systems psychology is not same as organizational/industrial psychology

When I first started working on systems psychology, I was often asked if it was the same as organizational/industrial psychology. However, it is not. In industrial psychology, we learn various aspects of behaviours in workplace settings. In fact, the word 'organization' defined in this branch of psychology does not consider the systemic approach. In chapter 2, I defined an organization as a workplace that works with systemic depth and breadth. Above all, in systems psychology, my main focus is not centred on human behaviour, rather I focus on how systems behave under different situations. Though I talk about human behaviour in depth, I define humans as system influencers—internal and external influencers as well as direct and indirect (forced) influences.

How are organizational and systems psychology different and why should we learn systems psychology? Relationships (both inter and intra) are also taken into account in systems psychology but these are centred on systems and influencers. However, I have used terms similar to those in other branches of psychology to ensure that studying this new field is not an isolated endeavour. However, every aspect is evaluated from a systemic lens. Each organization is chiefly made up of its people, but the fact is that you cannot study everyone's behaviour individually. Both psychologists and workplace managers know how difficult it is to predict human behaviour. Hence, with a human-focused approach, you cannot ensure organizational behaviour. It becomes very easy if you approach human behaviours through systems. Be it policy resistance or decision making, the systemic approach can become a game changer in organizational success.

Consider that you have 100 employees, 30 staff and 70 shop floor workers. Organizational psychology talks about a set of behaviours required in the workplace to get things done effectively and efficiently whereas systems psychology talks about how systems behave under the influence of those 100 employees, how indirect influencers (supervisors, managers, or top management) influence the system (through direct influencers or say shop floor workers) under different situations and studies the consequences (system feedback) so that we can rearrange the basic considerations to improve the system. Let's look at both once again to understand them in a little detail.

Continuously monitoring, controlling, and improving all your 100 employees is nearly impossible. At the same time, leaving them to their own will can put you at risk. It is like a double-edged sword hanging over your head. This difficulty is very severe in organizational psychology where you study people's behaviours in workplaces so that you can improve them. In contrast, in systems psychology, the behaviour of the system is studied and analyzed to understand influences, influencers, and situations for improvement. If you safeguard your system, everyone is automatically safe, individual effort is not necessary. This is what the verse from Srimad Bhagavatam says, "As pouring water on the root of a tree energizes the trunk, branches, twigs and everything else."

The true 'lean' in The Third Eye

True success is what you've achieved in contrast to what you could've achieved i.e. your potential.

To simplify the depth and breadth of systems psychology, I will take a familiar example of 'lean.' The world knows that lean means 'eliminating waste.' Though this is correct, when you look through the systemic eye (**The Third Eye**) this statement itself is *too lean.* We are limiting the true potential of the lean. In my work, I define lean as 'the scientific way of optimizing and synchronizing systems by using the least possible resources to produce great quality products or services.'

We all are given some resources in life, both in our professional and personal capacities. Success or happiness lies in how we use and manage the given resources. Gandhiji said, "The world has enough for everyone's needs but not everyone's greed." So, we must make proper use of the resources. Instead of focusing on the lean angle, look at the bigger picture and see how can you optimize and synchronize your systems to get the best from the least—The True Lean.

Why do systems produce errors?

Why do systems produce errors? Or, in other words, why do systems surprise us? We feel regretful when we read stories of heartbreaking accidents and disasters or see movies of great accidents like Titanic, the Chernobyl disaster, the Bhopal gas tragedy, the Challenger space shuttle disaster, and many others. We feel regret for those innocent victims but if you come to know how those systems were compromised before leading to accidents, how those influencers led those systems into disastrous mode you will say, "There's no surprise here, the disaster was obvious." The state or conditions those operators and influencers led their systems into was similar to unknowingly manifesting the disaster. I call such kinds of deliberate disasters an overestimation of certainty.

The Titanic captain overestimated that the ship had advanced safety features so he repeatedly kept on ignoring iceberg warnings and didn't reduce its speed even at that time of night. The chief engineer at Chernobyl overestimated what he knew about the reactors despite obvious signs of what was happening in the control room. NASA engineers and managers knew the problem yet they overestimated the safe launch and the result was the Challenger disaster.

Every story talks about overestimating certainty or overconfidence. Problems always lie in the systems but they may not have necessarily originated in them. Sometimes influencers influence the system and create compromises. Systems will surprise us on two occasions i.e. improper design of system structure and erroneous way of influencing great systems. Yet, if you want to prevent further damage, you need to work on systems alone, not on influencers. Why is that?

Why do we need to work on systems even if the influencers led the system to disaster? Because it is a foolproof method. They led those systems to disasters because those systems lacked defences. Whatever considerations we have taken into account while designing our systems are dynamic in nature. Your organizational structure, culture, people skills, customer profiles (new customers enter or old customers improve their working), and external environment such as markets, competitors, etc.—all change over time. When these considerations change, you have to analyze your systems to check whether your defences are adequate or not. When the Titanic was designed it was certified as the safest system but the defences were not adequate to defend it under the final conditions. The configurations done by the ship's operators were not in alignment with its defences.

In most instances, we are often in a state where we don't get expert operators, and even if we get some, we cannot guarantee that they will not negatively influence systems. They may deliberately compromise it (some air crashes happened because expert pilots deliberately carried out certain actions. They were called cockpit killers, for example, LAM 470 crash). So we must work on strengthening the system to enhance its defences further, to improve its error-proofing ability. Only systems can help us to error-proof themselves so that we achieve all four fundamental characteristics.

Though I believe that there is some human error component in most problems and accidents, I look at it differently. Throughout this book, I kept saying, that at the subconscious level we all are honest and we don't want to harm others intentionally. Yet, sometimes some people carry out deliberate acts. Though these are special cases, we should work on system structure and on improving defences to deal with such acts because it's a foolproof way to improve. You cannot know what someone else is thinking. Investigators of such deliberate crashes also recommend that airlines strengthen their systems. In addition to that, I would go one step further in **The Third Eye** and recommend 'building learning influencers.' A strong system along with learning influencers is the solution to handle even deliberate acts.

How to incorporate basic learning theories in systems design for error proofing? I will illustrate this through a classic example i.e. stick shaker in aeroplanes. Under certain conditions, like spatial disorientation, pilots cannot understand that the plane is going to stall until it is too late to do anything. The only way to protect the system is through the system itself i.e. designing it to understand systems behaviours. This stick shaker mechanism helps pilots to know that the plane is going to stall. Whatever systems you design, put in such warning mechanisms that are very basic to human learning so that your frontline people can understand the system's signals without any extra effort and take corrective actions.

Instead of giving day-long training sessions, creating this type of learning arrangement using various conditioning methods helps people learn better, easier, and quicker. Teach foolproofing methods to improve systems but teach them through learning.

How do you protect your systems from surprises?

As of now, I have worked on two ways to protect systems from surprises—confidence index analysis and conducting system audits. I have discussed the former in the previous chapter and will discuss the latter here. An audit doesn't mean using long checklists and filling them just for compliance purposes. Compliance does not necessarily save your systems, many times (chiefly in non-systemic cultures) it just masks the problems and does not solve them. Systems audit means identifying systems, intrinsic systems (to analyze defences better) and influencers and how that system has behaved in the recent past or the period between your last audit and the current one. An analysis of every erroneous behaviour can be done and improved if there are any gaps in defences. These types of audits can easily help you prevent surprises.

Another form of auditing widely practised today is the Layered Process Audit. Here the audit is done by auditors from different hierarchies such as supervisors, managers, HODs, executives, etc. This is another way to tap into the benefits of collective cognitive vibrations. Everyone has different observational skills and these can become significantly valuable when you involve higher levels (hierarchies). It solves two problems—the shop floor managers get opportunities to improve their workplace and the top management who usually sit in the board rooms and go through financial figures get to know what is going on in the workplace. Hence their expectations become more realistic. Aspiration is good but over-aspiration hurts people down the line.

When does the system suffer?

Systems suffer under various conditions, mainly when there are learning barriers in the company. Apart from them, systems suffer under two more conditions:

- **When an individual's interests get bigger than the collective's:** In the previous chapter, I discussed the One Company One Voice campaign. The purpose of this campaign is to make sure that there is a shared vision and that company interests are more than individual interests and expectations. If you find anyone with contrary behaviour, follow the sack or shackle approach, but do not let the system suffer.
- **Expectations beyond systemic requirements:** This creates forceful influences like corruption. You get paid as per your roles and responsibilities, but if you start expecting beyond what you deserve such as accepting money in immoral ways, it leads to corruption. This was seen in the example of the Kolkata client and the system suffered.

When the system is satisfied everyone is satisfied, conversely, when the system suffers everyone suffers. A company is bigger than all of us. If you show interest in saving only your seat neither your seat nor the company will be saved. On the other hand, if you work to save the company then everyone's seat will be saved automatically. Stop the save my seat campaign.

How do systems learn their lessons?

By this time, you know how systems learn their lessons, it is through people who are working for the system but that is easier said than done. Although systems learn from their influencers, their learning pattern is very different. For example, when a company is asked about standardization, its first approach is to prepare standard operating procedures or SOPs. Preparing and following procedures is the first and easiest way to start building systems, whether it's a product-centred or company-centred system. Also, systems learn and remember most of their earlier lessons through procedural memory. Procedural memory is non-declarative memory since it is hard to explain to others. Employees work but when you ask them how they do it, they find it difficult to explain. Again, this is not a linear approach, there are many other factors to be considered, but still, it plays a large role in the transformation of a company into an organization. Another important advantage of this procedural memory is that it helps a company deal with policy resistance and strengthens the system.

Systems psychologist

I can directly compare learning influencers to systems psychologists since they solve problems in a systemic way and understand the system's behaviour. Some additional things to be understood are included in this section.

The task of a psychologist is to understand and predict behaviour. In the same way, the task of a systems psychologist is to understand and predict the system's behaviour under various influences/influencers.

Like a human, a system too has behavioural components. If you want to understand a human, you must first understand his/her behaviours. Behaviours are our mental patterns that map our actions, what we do and why we do it. If you want to make a child a good scientist, you will start teaching him about science from his childhood, helping him experiment with theories and getting him admission into an appropriate school and college. Our formal education provides us with certain insights and behaviours and a basic understanding of the world we live in.

What to learn and where to learn it from is the most important skill for every learner, you cannot learn everything from everywhere. Formal education teaches you behaviours and develops mental models.

System psychologists generate hypotheses about systems behaviours which can be categorized into how influencers influence systems to exhibit specific behaviours and in turn how influencers handle those behaviours. If I put these things in a loop or a systemic model, it can become either a virtuous cycle or a vicious cycle. A virtuous cycle is one that has a negative feedback loop. It balances itself and is a good system which has three fundamental characteristics. A vicious cycle is one that has a positive feedback loop resulting in a never-ending growth cycle (self-reinforcing) which destroys itself after some time. A classic example of this vicious cycle is the Chernobyl disaster. They used the RBMK[9] reactor which is a graphite-moderated water-cooled reactor which under that situation created a vicious cycle and caused the system to stall and explode. To avoid this vicious cycle, nuclear reactors are now designed with water-cooled and water-moderated technology so that as and when water reduces as a coolant the reaction is also slowed. This creates a negative feedback loop, a balancing behaviour or a virtuous cycle.[10]

---

9 RBMK - Reaktor bolshoy moshchnosti kanalnyy, high-power channel-type reactor

10 Considering the dynamic nature of systems, even the positive loops will operate as virtuous cycles sometimes and vice versa. But, those peculiar behaviours are largely dependent on

What happens if influencers influence the system negatively by giving false input which causes erroneous output? I hypothesized that this could be due to a lack of awareness or overconfidence (overestimating certainty). Influencers can further ignore the system signals and keep supplying the same erroneous inputs hoping that the system will stabilize soon (escalation of commitment behaviour). This kind of situation creates a vicious cycle that either stalls the system or keeps generating errors. This is what I tested in the example of the aluminium extrusion in chapter 4. Though I got the result that I theorized—stall or keep generating errors—I still have some more system variables to test, so I cannot say that my experiment proved all of my hypotheses.

Why is systemic study so important though it remains a widely neglected field? Throughout my studies in engineering or research methods or system thinking or design thinking and various branches of psychology, I consistently found systematic patterns and multiple errors that essentially damage the essence of the predictions. For a researcher studying the correlation between two variables, the observations do not make any sense when a third unnoticed variable influences and sidetracks the entire prediction. Similarly, a researcher studying some behaviours through surveys finds a third component that may involve and influence the entire outcome of the survey such ill-influenced results would be of no use. This unexpected involvement of the third component is very difficult to predict unless we see the whole picture i.e. a systemic view. In my investigations, I repeatedly faced this issue but I always took cautious steps to verify the components involved and the variables being influenced. A cause-and-effect relationship is not always linear as seen in normal non-systemic problem-solving methodologies. Establishing one such relationship doesn't guarantee the solution either. This is one of the reasons why I developed the factor categorization method. The NICE analysis helps to review components and feedback analysis is an excellent way to take the system back to the scene. All this seems widely stretched but when you apply this systemic method of solving problems to real problems, you'll see how simple it is. Instilling the understanding of this simple, natural, and scientific method deep into our minds is one of the purposes of systems psychology.

Observations and experiments: The weapons of psychologists

Observation and experimentation are important tools that every psychologist uses to learn behaviours. This is called the empirical method of learning. Psychology is very much close to generative intelligence. You hardly ever heard that psychologists are trained, they learn through empirical methods i.e. observation and experimentation.

I follow the four-step approach of DO IT, proposed by psychologist Scott Geller. Define, Observe, Intervene, and Test which is very familiar to most psychologists. Though there are dozens of other methods, I follow this most often as I mainly study applied

the factors involved and relationships between them. For our first level of reference, we should study positive loops as vicious cycles and negative ones as virtuous cycles. Systems are highly dynamic and that's why systems thinking is a very special skill that requires generative intelligence.

behaviours. Set up some hypotheses (define some theories) and prepare procedures to observe the behaviours as defined in the target or hypotheses. Behaviourism in psychology talks about actions that can be observed and measured, behavioural study means observing and measuring actual behaviours and comparing them with expected behaviours as per the system's necessity. Then one can intervene to change it as expected by the process or systemic necessities. Even in systems psychology, I study human behaviours as the system behaviour is influenced by both direct and indirect influencers. If I want to intervene to change systems behaviours then I must work on developing predictable frontal system interactions and then using them to change behaviours. The third step is intervention. In the end, there is a test or experiment to know how the changed behaviours are performing. This step helps me plan for my next level of study, situational awareness.

In January 2023, I investigated a failure at one of my clients. After work, I wanted to sow a seed of learning by conducting an experiment. The experiment was about obviousness and substantiveness. I handed all 34 participants a page of numbers from one to three hundred which were spelt out. The task was to identify the number of 'a's in it within 2 minutes. I hypothesized that people in senior positions often fall into substantive traps. The same was true here. The ones who had a good aptitude made mistakes and the ones who were poor at statistics made no mistakes at all! Aptitude guys know that the occurrence of 'a' happens only when we reach a thousand, so they just checked the first and last word. When they found that the task began with one and ended with three hundred, they said zero occurrences. In fact, I had made two deliberate errors at 172 (one-hundrad-seventy-two) and 219 (two-hundred-ninetean). Initially, I made it very clear that it was an experiment to observe things carefully. They overestimated the certainty that I had made no spelling mistakes, but when I am about to test substantiveness I can make deliberate mistakes as I want to check their observational skills. However, I had given them enough time but they wasted the minutes by failing to notice the errors. When someone asks you to observe things, neither overestimate things nor underestimate things. This observational skill is so powerful that you can get at least 80% of results just by substantive observation. I have data to prove that it can go even to 90%. Quality professionals call this the poison cake test. In my work, I call this the obviousness-substantiveness test since I conduct these studies with a wider scope to cover systems and influencers' behaviours.

Generalization challenge

When I started working on systems psychology, I used to think that generalization and naturalization were major challenges to this concept. But, by the time I finished foundational work on revealing system structure in terms of 6 basic considerations and three fundamental characteristics (I added the fourth, self-learning later) it was very clear that every system is different in its structure as the combinations in their considerations hardly ever match. Hence every system has a built-in competitive advantage as well as uniqueness. These wider considerations make systems thinking highly generalized and naturalized so that the concept can be applied anywhere and for anything, from a small start-up to a global organization, from a shoe manufacturer to a space shuttle or a software developer.

I talked about generalization in chapter 2, but here I want to give a quick test way to know if you are facing a generalization challenge in your company.

As an owner, a director, or an executive, ask yourself questions such as, "Can my team manage tough situations in my absence? Can my team handle customers without my involvement when they face a serious complaint?"

If your answer is no or not always, then you are facing a generalization challenge in your system. It's time to work on the system structure.

A generalization challenge affects the company in many ways. The most important one is that as the owner you need to be involved in every single activity of your company. This aspect drains your energy and makes you ineffective at other important tasks like growing the company (attention residue effect). Some other effects are that customers feel less confident about your company, you start feeling that systems are of no use and work only for compliance, you may adopt multiple systems in order to satisfy individual customers, your employees may behave irresponsibly and kill the learning culture, the system may become the victim of policy resistance, and many more.

Your journey to excellence starts the moment you understand and admit I'm at the wrong place.

How can you build foolproof systems?

If you want to build foolproof systems, understanding how systems learn lessons, how systems behave under various influences and how policy resistance affects systems performance is very necessary.

In the previous sections, I discussed error-proofing systems and working on the system structure so that you keep influence points in check. That works well and there are still some more actions that need to be taken.

- **Ensure education:** Educate your employees, especially those workers who are the first point of influence on your systems and intrinsic systems. Their inputs mean a lot to the system. Educate them and through their input strengthen the system
- **Use the sack or shackle:** It's always better to remove weeds, but sometimes you cannot sack them so use the system's structure to shackle them
- **Implement Confidence Index Analysis:** Use this method to improve the decision-making ability of your people and let every major decision pass through the system, the **third eye**
- **Avoid all the barriers to learning**: Help the workplace become a hub for organizational learning
- **Develop learning influencers:** They are the people who can take you on an uplifting journey. Never consider influencers as just employees. They are people with a system in their hearts and heads. They can help you build a solid error-proof system

- **Use the four-step framework**: Use it for solving problems and never forget to write lessons learned and use those lessons in strengthening systems
- **Launch learning influencers programme:** Especially the One Company One Voice and the Problem Solving Campaign and then form a problem solvers forum for long-term system improvements. This forum is like the parliament, they review problems and solutions in a systemic light and help the company revise policies and system structure
- **Share companywide awareness of generative intelligence:** Become three-year-old children and learn by experiments and testing things. Their world is beautiful because they learn and do not get trained
- **Battle-test your company to face changing conditions:** Policy resistance can be dealt with through this technique as well. Provide exposure to varying situations like customer audits by having frequent internal audits and system reviews. It is better if it is done by the learning influencers. They know how to look for things that are not ordinarily visible and they know how to listen to the voice that is generally inaudible
- **Implement Eisenhower's time management matrix:** Do this strictly, especially in project management. The more problems you solve in the project development stage the more lessons you'll learn and learnings are the true assets of any company or organization. Nobody can steal them. There are many possibilities and the majority of the time, once the tasks go into the urgent box, you will try to forcefully influence your first-line system influencers, leading to system compromise and suffering. You'll try to uphold your self-interest rather than the system's interest to save your seat. Even though you complete the tasks in the urgent box you have failed because you are poisoning your system.

All those people who achieved something beyond their capacity have one thing in common. They all have the special ability to learn things quickly. I teach this ability with the acronym LTQ—Learn Things Quickly. We all have the same number of hours in a day, the faster you learn the earlier you start and you'll be able to reach a height which is beyond the reach of ordinary people.

Systems assessment

I recommend that businesses and professionals study and understand systems psychology. I also suggest that businesses should assess their systems to know how they are getting affected. Whether you're building systems or reassessing the 6 basic considerations for improvements, the systems assessment helps you to know the reality. To simplify this assessment task, I have made a checklist, a non-exhaustive one, of things that point to the need for assessment.

- Repeated complaints from customers
- Feeling a strong need to hire consultants to run your business
- Increasing internal rejections
- Sudden improvements in quality. This is an indication that people have learned to hide problems. But they are managing messes, not solving problems.

Remember, having no problems is a bigger risk than not solving problems unless you are a learning organization. Overnight improvement is a scam

- People think that following systemic practices is a burden and a waste of time and money
- Repeated system compliance issues from external and internal auditors
- Spending too much on systems but not sure whether it is worth it or not
- Stagnation of wrong people and rapid flow of right people
- Supply chain pollution—poor suppliers, last-minute deliveries, over or under inventory, fluctuation in inventory
- Corrupt hands at work (most of the time, you may be unaware of this, but the behaviour of the corrupt can tell you everything)

If you have any of these problems, then study systems psychology and work on developing learning influencers.

Grit: The power of passion and perseverance

To know and not to do is not yet to know.

–Zen saying

LTQ is important for success but just learning doesn't help unless you stick to those lessons and put them to use. Angela Lee Duckworth, a psychologist and the author of *Grit* mentions a characteristic in her TED talk to predict success.

She says, "It's not just learning quickly or easily but sticking to those lessons for long-term goals is what brings success."

She calls this characteristic grit. Many recent studies and research have proved that having a high IQ or Intelligence Quotient doesn't guarantee your success. There are many other factors to be considered for achieving success. Even psychologists changed the method used to calculate IQ.

Angela defines grit as, "Passion and perseverance for very long-term goals, it is sticking with your future and working hard to make that future a reality."

This is the basic difference between training and learning. Learning means connecting lessons to your daily work and updating your knowledge, sticking to your lessons, having the courage to think for the future and developing the determination required to transform your lessons into reality.

Toyota: The true learning organization

The purpose that drives me to work on systems psychology is to educate professionals, companies, and organizations about systems behaviours. During my initial days of working on the systems psychology concept, I closely studied books and papers written on systemic organizations. I would like to mention one of those here. It is none other than Toyota, the organization that changed the concept of quality forever. I learnt that quality is psychology from this organization. The Toyoda family or the early leaders of Toyota never established quality as a strategy. Neither was it one of the departments that worked for systems compliance like almost all the companies worldwide did in those days (sadly, even to this day). Nor did they put quality as a framework in their business playbook. Toyota ensured that quality became their philosophy and this was embedded deeply into their psychology.

I have studied many books on the organization but 'The Toyota Way' stands out. A quick first point of reference about this book is that the author has mentioned the word strategy 7 times, principle 289 times, and system a whopping 571 times (I am referring to the first edition). This shows how Toyota works. The author, Jeffrey Liker, teaches Toyota's approach to excellence in the form of 14 principles divided into 4 parts. All 14 of them circle the system, namely the famous Toyota Production System. The 4 parts are[11] philosophy (long-term systems thinking), process (struggle to flow value to each customer), people (respect, challenge, and grow your people and partners toward a vision of excellence) and problem-solving (think and act scientifically to improve toward a desired future).

If you study all 4 parts and 14 principles closely, you'll find that they all loop around those 6 basic considerations I explained earlier in this book. Through these principles, they have achieved all four fundamental characteristics of a system and are a live example of a learning organization. Toyota is credited for the quality revolution so I always had this question, "Why didn't they name it Toyota Quality System instead of Toyota Production System?" The reason is simple, yet again, for them quality was not a strategy, department or framework, it was in their people's psychology and they wanted quality to be in their culture so that whatever they do will be of the highest in class. When it comes to improvement, quality is psychology.

Following their industrial success, many of the Japanese words became synonymous with the practices industries follow, words like Kaizen (change for better), Poka-Yoke (foolproof), Hoshin Kanri (policy deployment) and many more. To give a contrasting view, Kaizen is a scientific and psychological term. We study this in 'shaping and chaining' under operant conditioning wherein behaviours are shaped through rewarding each small step or improvement. The principle of shaping is very simple, it states that 'consistent small changes lead to a huge leap in the long term.' Consistency is the key here. Instead of rewarding the final result, recognize every small improvement. This makes a lot of sense in shaping target behaviours and awakens the desire in frontline workers to keep improving the process and the system. Eventually, these small improvements form a chain and make it easy to learn even complex behaviours. Like this, I have analyzed every single learning organization's practices under my systems psychology research and uncovered a lot of lessons that the world needs to know.

How have those practices worked for those organizations and how can we generalize those lessons for wider use and applications so that we can have several learning organizations? In my research journey and career, I've met many companies who tried to copy-paste practices of other successful organizations but have only ended up in system traps. Please remember that what worked for them may not work for you, unless you prepare your system for those practices. Every system is unique. Great systems have this built-in capability. Learn the lessons and then work on building systems.

11 The Toyota Way by Jeffrey K. Liker Second edition, McGraw Hill 2021

I have some differences and resentment over the way the authors who wrote about Toyota mentioned problem-solving methods and their usage of the word training instead of learning. I use some of the best techniques like set-based concurrent engineering to teach design thinking and highlight the importance of project management over design capabilities. I have seen companies seriously think about enhancing design capability for growth but give less priority, or even ignore, the importance of project management. At the end of the day, they fail to reap the full benefits of the change. Project management plays a crucial role in the journey of building systems, becoming a learning organization, and ultimately achieving the third E, excellence.

I want to give you an exercise here. Find as much learning material as you can about hoshin kanri and write about how you can generalize those lessons for your company.[12]

Situational awareness

A fair number of my classmates are in the armed forces and the central and state police forces. Whenever we meet we discuss our work, what we do, how our routine is, and other things.

On a lighter note, we often criticize each other and they tell me, "You are the fault finder, earning money by finding faults in others."

I tell them, "You people fire tax money to the rocks and in the air."

That was because we are close but we respect each other's professions. As you know, a close relationship means having a conversation beyond professionalism. But to be honest, I have always been regretful over my comments to our protectors after every such criticism. As an auditor, investigator, and systems builder, I am well aware that every bullet those soldiers fire, even in the air or to the hills, is protecting our country. When an enemy stands before you suddenly, no amount of classroom training can help you. You cannot fire even a single bullet at the right place using even the most advanced guns. Awareness of the situation is essential and we should have a mental map in our mind, and prepare ourselves not just physically but psychologically as well.

Like people, even systems experience various situations and their associated behaviours depending on the influencers' inputs. Whether it's a system or a human, behaviours are influenced by the situation. If we want to control the behaviour, then it's necessary to control the situation or at least be aware of the situations because many times we cannot control the situations. I don't know what they teach in organizational behaviour courses, but I would be happy if they taught systems and how influences affect behaviour. Identifying the problem is a bigger problem than solving it.

Battle-test your employees and your business continuity plan just to ensure you have air to breathe in the worst times. You may have well-educated forces along with multiple business continuity plans in your playbook, but if they weren't battle tested or not designed for the worst possible situations, none of them is useful, and they won't save you in crisis. To be a good runner, you have to learn to manage your breath, otherwise, you cannot finish the race.

---

12 Note: Do not search the internet, rather study books. If you want to generalize lessons of hoshin kanri then it is not about strategy, it is completely about the system.

Every serious issue I have investigated and studied has occurred because of a chain of events. It's nearly impossible that a single error could cause a serious problem. There has to be a combination of factors that can compromise a system, either due to wrong system design or false system influences. When a lethal combination of influences caused by the situations and influencers creates all the necessary conditions for something tragic to occur, I have learned two lessons from each such investigation and study—what you should do to avoid it and what you should do if you happen to be in one.

It's always easier to blame system operators because it's what is obviously visible to a layman's eyes i.e. a non-systemic person. You have to accept that if you go on blaming the humans involved, you'll never be able to solve problems or prevent one. Whatever the incident, no matter its severity, I always look for systems. How did the system respond when there was an error or something not right was in sight? Again, it gives you two things, either there was no system signal to tell that there has been an error or even after finding an error the influencer(s) did nothing. If no signal means the system's structure is not designed for that objective and if influencers did nothing that means they weren't aware of how to manage situations and handle the systems. When you reach this conclusion, you arrive at both the cause as well as the solution. That's what my four-step problem-solving framework is all about—improving the system and providing situational awareness to system operators.

I would like to cite an example. I have seen companies failing audits because of people's lack of awareness or more precisely, lack of situational awareness. One such experience was when I got a project in Pune in August 2020, just a few months after the COVID-19 lockdown was lifted. One of my ex-suppliers failed a customer audit 4 times and the customer sent an email stating that he would give one last chance to clear the audit or else the supplier would be dropped from the business considerations and he could not allocate auditing resources endlessly. Since one of the directors knew me well, he called me one afternoon and explained the situation.

To prepare myself, I asked him for some details and conducted a gap analysis through a video call. After that, I took a week to make some preparations and travelled to Pune. While skimming through their systems, I understood the problem, which was simple. But since it had been ignored, it had almost strangled them. Instead of the documents, I worked on a systemic approach. The people were entirely unaware of audits. When customers came they became overly stressed and couldn't even exhibit their good practices. This happens to everyone. Just think how you would feel when you are asked to give a speech on stage without prior information. Wouldn't you feel as if the earth is quaking? The public speaking coaching industry is in operation because of this one problem—situational awareness, especially stage fear.

Customers always try to find gaps. This is not to show that you are weak and they are smart, but they want you to improve so that they can be confident. System is confidence. But, it's your responsibility and priority to show your good practices and teach customers if you are following anything unique. I learned many things from my suppliers. I stayed 5 days with them for the preparation. Every day, I audited their practices so that I could prepare them for the final exam—their customer audit. I conducted 3 rounds of auditing and exposed them to various possible situations. I prepared a report and discussed it with the director. Initially, he was unhappy with my remarks, but at the end of the report, he smiled and thanked me. I shared a checklist with him and asked him to audit his processes at least once a month to maintain this awareness. Two weeks later, they passed the customer audit easily.

This is one of many such instances where I have clearly seen how important it is to create situational awareness in your people. Even if you are a manager, without planning, if I ask you to come and give a speech on any topic of your interest, you'll stutter while speaking or will take unnoticed pauses in between. If this happens to a manager, then how can you expect your workers on the shop floor to face situations they are never aware of and yet succeed? Facing any situation needs prior awareness and practice. These simple situational awareness practices can help your people become psychologically fit for any situation.

Almost a year ago, as part of my psychology studies, I went to a blind school. I wanted to know how they teach blind children. I wanted to learn deeper lessons, not what we find in books or over the internet. I always believed that you can search on Google and research in your mind. I am not the guy who sits before the internet all day and conducts research. On the contrary, I study concepts, make theories, write hypotheses, conduct experiments, collect and analyze data in various ways to look for interrelationships and intra-relationships, map the data, develop models, and then write reports. That's the reason what I do or write is rarely available on the internet or in any other books, my research takes place in my mind.

I spent an entire day with 3-4 teachers and had wonderful conversations. One of my questions was, "How do you teach these children to walk? If you blindfold me and ask me to walk 100 steps, of course, I can walk but cannot maintain a pattern of steps. They will be largely and sparsely scattered. How do you make them ready to face the world? I have seen some of the blind people achieve extraordinary feats." I had made that visit to learn more about how generative intelligence works in blind persons but it turned into a situational awareness learning session for me.

That middle-aged teacher told me, "We don't teach them walking or writing. All we teach them is confidence. You cannot maintain balance with a blindfold because you don't need to. You have eyes, you know your eyes are blinded temporarily, so you don't acquire that confidence. But for these children, their blindness is their life, they don't have any other option. All we do is build confidence."

Another teacher said, "You may have heard some people saying, teachers become eyes for blind students. No, we don't become their eyes, they have eyes already."

This confused me, so I asked for clarification. That school headmistress called a girl and tapped her shoulder and she explained, "See, we have two types of eyes. The first type of eyes or eyesight is gross, which you and I have and use to see things. Another type of eye or eyesight is subtle. It is called the internal eye. This is weak in you and me but very strong in blind children. It is the greatest gift of God to them. We teach them to strengthen this subtle eyesight but we cannot acquire it."

In the evening, when I was about to leave, another girl came to greet me. She didn't have a walking stick but she didn't miss her step. She walked straight up to me and said, "Thank you, sir. You came all the way to listen to our stories. This is a gift from us."

She gave me a colourful flower, an orchid, a flower whose colour she can never explain. When that 14-year-old blind girl gave me the flower, I might have cursed God. I became blind despite having eyes (tears blinded my vision). I thanked her and everyone else for their amazing confidence.

At the gate, I asked another teacher, "How confident she was! She walked like she wasn't blind."

"Shiva, have you noticed? We always call them physically handicapped or physically challenged. We should never say that they are handicapped. They are physically handicapped but mentally stronger than all of us. They are physically challenged but mentally they challenge all of us. You are here to learn the psychology of blind people. But did you know that every blind student is a psychologist? They have their world. You may say they cannot see the colours of this world but they have their colour. We cannot imagine their life, but they have to live."

I learned from that visit the role that awareness plays in our lives. The teachers teach blind children awareness through words and they, who can never see, develop mental models in their minds. They develop pictures of various situations and through questions they get their models tested. This awareness and situational clarification builds confidence in those students that we, the people with gross eyesight, can never imagine. Actually, I made that visit as part of my organizational learning research. I had hypothesized that the education given to the blind is a type of constructive learning. Their teachers train them and whatever they describe is converted into mental pictures by the students and leads to the construction of their knowledge.

If that is true, then how are students different? I have seen some students are highly successful and some others are barely aware of their surroundings. These differences tell a different theory. The intelligence of blind people is not necessarily the constructive type. They too have generative intelligence.

Think for a minute, if those teachers can teach situational awareness to those blind children, then why can't you do that for your employees? Why can't you build confidence in your employees? It's not difficult if you follow the procedures and practices of organizational learning.

The purpose of the Third Eye: Creating learning influencers

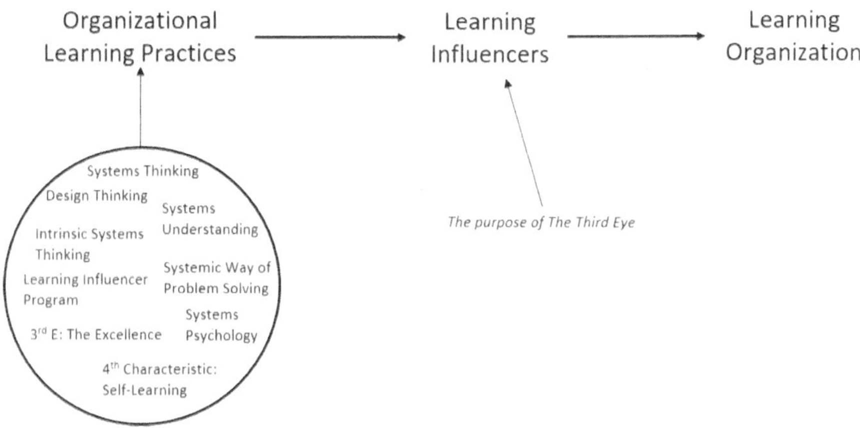

Figure 7.1

Organizational learning is a set of practices that creates learning influencers and they are the ones who take an ordinary organization to a learning organization embodying the 4th fundamental characteristic of a system i.e. self-learning. Creating such learning influencers is the purpose of the **third eye**.

In scientific settings, theories are the frameworks for explaining various events or processes and hypotheses are testable predictions derived from theories. The four-step framework that I presented in this book fits this definition and explains the process we need to follow to arrive at a fundamental solution.

What is the difference between a symptomatic solution and a fundamental solution? A symptomatic solution acts as a stop-gap option to deal with the symptom such as a cold bath when you have a fever to reduce your body temperature. Doing so may reduce your body temperature, but it doesn't solve the main problem. Actually, you don't know the real problem at all, all you know is the symptom of the problem i.e. the fever. Bathing in cold water worsens the situation even further as the pathogens in your body become more active (a side-effect of the symptomatic solution). Fever is not the problem, in fact, it is a defence mechanism of our body to fight against the pathogens within it. In the same way, even in our professional problems, we should never focus on symptom-centred solutions. Focus follows attention. If you define the problem up front you'll set your attention on that and automatically you will find things comparable to your defined problem. In reality, you need to identify what errors have taken place in the system and find solutions for that systemic problem i.e. a fundamental solution. It is good if you work on both product and organization-centred systems, it makes the system even stronger. You can use the Swiss cheese model for this intrinsic systems defence analysis.

The following diagram is derived by placing the **third eye** in the four-step framework.

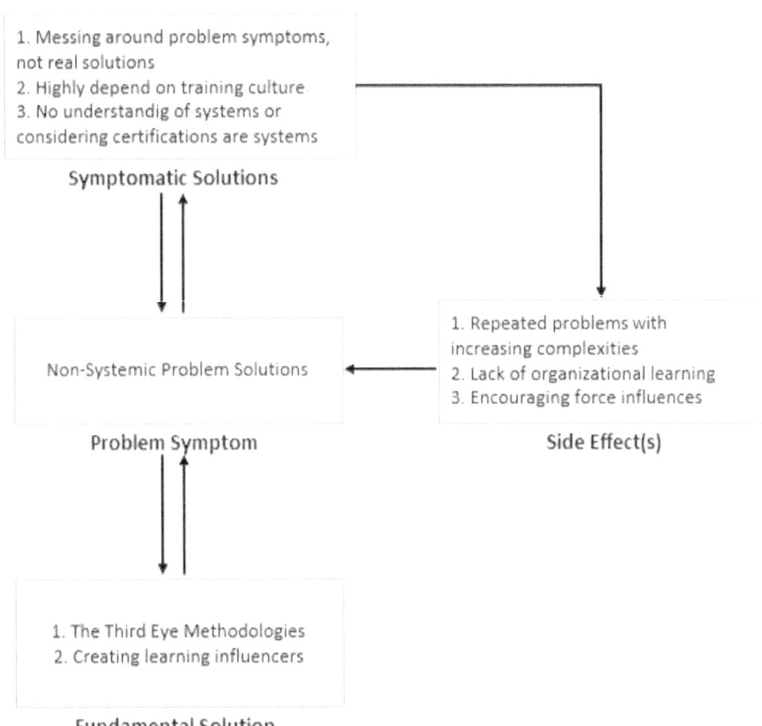

Four-Step Framework	
Symptom(s)	Repeated problems with increasing complexities
Concern(s)	Methodologies used to solve problems, systems structure
Problem(s)	Non-systemic problem solutions
Cause/Solution	Use Third Eye methodologies, create learning culture by following organizational learning practices, encourage generative intelligence

Figure 7.2

Brief overview of some global disasters

In this section, we will see some of the world's worst disasters and accidents just to recall our understanding till now.

"The school of failure is most effective for learning but the school of disasters is a costly school."

Without going into much detail, we will see some necessary facts about four cases, the Titanic disaster, the Bhopal gas tragedy, the Challenger space shuttle explosion, and the Chernobyl disaster. I will put the Chernobyl disaster and then the aluminium bracket failure into the Swiss cheese model.

Why is organizational learning important and what do these tragedies teach us? The one thing I realized from these four major disasters and hundreds of others is that we often fail to see the signals of upcoming tragedies. For example, the operators and engineers in the control room of Chernobyl led an entire continent (Europe) to the brink of destruction, the captain of the Titanic kept ignoring the ice warnings all along, the managers of the shuttle launch programme ignored what engineers were saying and the workers' were largely unaware of their work in Bhopal chemical factory. This is how the school of disaster becomes the costliest institution for all of us. We should learn to prevent them from happening again. We should see every incident in the light of the system and assess how these incidents could have been avoided along with learning lessons. Learning lessons is necessary but not at the cost of destruction.

Titanic: The unsinkable

I often think about why the Titanic, the unsinkable ship, sank on its maiden voyage. People often say that it was because of the mega-iceberg! They also quote many scientific theories. I always refute their claims as the ship did not sink due to any of those reasons.

For over a century, scientists and engineers across the world have investigated the causes of this accident. Dozens of new regulatory practices have been established to prevent such incidents from happening in the future. The iceberg theory is one among the many, 10% of it was above water and 90% below. But instead of all these theories, I think that it sank because it was in the wrong hands. The people who were in the control room i.e. influencers did not handle the system properly, they influenced it negatively and kept ignoring all the danger signals.

On April 10, 1912, RMS Titanic commenced its maiden and unfortunately last voyage from Southampton, England to its destination New York, United States. However, it did not reach its intended destination. Some reports say that from April 11th to 14th, it received nearly 20 ice warnings (a radio signal mechanism to alert other ships). It was captained by Edward Smith who ignored these signals and did not even reduce the ship's speed. He wanted to be the fastest ship to reach New York.

We will see a list of events we can use to learn lessons for our **third eye**

- On April 10th, 1912, the Titanic commenced its maiden and unfortunately, last journey

- From April 11th 1912 till just one hour before the crash, the ship received ice warnings, the symptoms of the upcoming problem. The iceberg was not the issue
- Captain Edward Smith, ignored the warnings. Ignoring system signals can be costly, fatal, and disastrous
- Finally, on April 14th 1912, close to midnight, the ship struck an iceberg. The steering operator panicked and steered the ship in the opposite direction. Instead of escaping, the ship collided with it early, a clear example of a lack of situational awareness. The operator was not aware of managing tough situations. If he had, he would have reduced the severity of the collision significantly.

Bhopal gas tragedy

Why did this gas tragedy happen? The worst industrial disaster in India happened on December 3rd 1984, in Bhopal, Madhya Pradesh. It wasn't because of a lack of government regulations, it was because of the mishandling of the system by the company. As professionals, the place we work is where we spend the majority of our waking hours. Many of us come home just to get some rest and go back refreshed for the next day's exercises. If this is the case, then why don't we follow systems where we work? Why do we keep ignoring safety signals? I have met people who say that gloves weighing 45 gms, helmets weighing 250 gms and goggles weighing 35 gms are heavy, but believe me, you are not rigid enough to survive if a machine loves your hand or head. In just a fraction of a second, it can rip your body parts off.

Key happenings which led up to the disaster were

- In 1980, Union Carbide India Limited (UCIL) was allowed to locally produce MIC (Methyl Isocyanate), a dangerous chemical. It used to be imported earlier. There were no precautions taken. The decision was just to save costs without a risk analysis
- The workers were completely unaware of the dangers of the chemicals they were working with. Because of this, the workers ignored a leak as they thought it was a small one but this ignorance had disastrous consequences. I talked about people skills under designing system structure (one among the 6 basic considerations) and I talked about creating awareness in AIDA model. The first letter in the AIDA talks about awareness. It helps influencers handle the systems appropriately. Without awareness, you cannot build error-proof systems.
- The interesting thing was that even doctors didn't know how to treat the patients who were sick after inhaling the chemical. They didn't know which chemical they were exposed to and gave patients oxygen to aid in their breathing and this further aggravated the situation as MIC had an accelerated reaction with oxygen
- Chemicals were stored in a capacity above the allowed maximum safe limit. This was a clear overriding of standard safety features, a non-systemic practice

- The chemical tank was damaged as it had not been maintained properly. In fact, there were a series of maintenance issues in this disaster, maintenance was breached everywhere
- Lastly, when the leak happened, the company did not alert the surrounding area. Did they want to hide this disaster which was already in the air?

Who was responsible? More than an accident, it was a deliberate act supported by multiple stakeholders. The cost of ignoring the system's signals can be massive. Investigations into this accident were reported in terms of chemical reactions. But it was due to system failure. Nobody looked at this through the systemic eye. Keep the legal battles aside. As system learners and system thinkers, we cannot blame the company, the workers or the government, it was the complete failure of the system. What lessons can other chemical manufacturers learn from this in terms of systems? That is the question.

Challenger space shuttle

Why did the Challenger explode just 73 seconds after lift-off? It was not because of the failure of an O-ring. On January 28, 1986, the Challenger space shuttle on its voyage to space exploded just 73 seconds after lift-off. Some important circumstances surrounding the disaster are outlined below.

- The space shuttle's solid rocket boosters were built by Morton Thiokol. They learned that there was a problem in its design in its 1977 test, the tang-and-clevis bent away from each other, reducing the pressure on the O-rings. This allowed the combustion gasses to damage the O-rings: Thiokol persuaded NASA and said that it was not desirable but was acceptable and the managers at NASA agreed! An example of overestimating certainty or overconfidence.
- The NASA certification committee requested further tests to test joint integrity and even asked the team to do testing with only one O-ring. The launch managers decided that it was sufficient and no further tests were required. If this was the response to a request by the certification committee, then what is the credibility of that committee? Was the certification just a formality? Or just a compliance requirement? In the second chapter, we have already seen that systems get compromised because of our blind beliefs. You cannot ensure a good system by just having certifications or a certifications committee. They should have the authority to execute their responsibility and the entire company or organization should work on the principle of reciprocity. If there's a systemic requirement then work on it to fulfill it. Do not overestimate the certainty.
- Design modifications were done and despite the availability of modified solid rocket boosters in which this O-ring issue was resolved, Thiokol continued to use an unmodified version. This represented a lack of team consensus. The design was not evaluated or discussed within the team and if Thiokol was not ready to use a modified version, then why did NASA spend money on it? It shows a lack of basic design thinking practices. A desirability-viability-feasibility test was not conducted.

- The primary O-ring was found eroded in November 1981 launch and ignored
- As early as four years before the accident, in 1982, NASA rated this O-ring failure as high severity. If this was the case, why didn't NASA test with the O-ring installation so that joint integrity can be verified, as requested by its committee? Knowing but not taking any action similar to not knowing.
- In 1984, 2 years before the accident, in a test O-ring scorching was observed but the Marshall Space Center said that there was no action required. The signal was once again ignored.
- In 1985, the NASA project managers placed launch constraints and there were to be no shuttle launches if there were any issues in the highly critical items. But still, the NASA management allowed deviation from this decision as they were unaware of the constraints: If project managers were asked to hold and subsequently the management deviated, why didn't they pass a severity call to the management? Both project managers and top management played the compliance card i.e., 'I did my job'.

This series of events shows the ignorance of systemic practices, they knew that failure was likely but nobody acted. Initially, Thiokol's engineers said not desirable but acceptable when they were questioned. Later Thiokol said that they should not launch but NASA managers allowed it. There was a complete breach of the system. O-ring failure was not the reason, it was system failure. Human errors were largely involved but to control humans we need to put systems in place. That's why in the entire book I keep emphasizing the 6 basic considerations for designing your system structure so that you will have a better system in place. We can't control human errors directly, it can only be done with systemic approaches.

Despite all the advanced simulator-based training, the top three causes of airline accidents are attributed to human error. Piloting error accounts for 50% of those. This number combined with the other human-related causes (crew mistakes and traffic controlling errors) can easily surpass 60%. This shows how important it is to have a system that ensures influencers influence it positively.

Not only in aviation but in any industry the proportion of human error is significantly high and every remedial action involves training the operators. If training could have solved the problems, then it wouldn't have arrived in the first place. Training can never be the solution. My recommendations include providing situational awareness to your people so that they can behave as per the situation and strengthening systemic practices. If you are blaming the workers or people or the machine, you are missing the systemic eye, the **third eye**. Look through this extra eye and you'll see a different picture. I don't say that there will be no problems but repetitions will be zero. Most importantly, you'll learn lessons at almost *zero cost* (human cost).

If you study closely, you'll find that disasters are not accidents. They are waiting in the lobby, waiting in the hope that someone will invite them in to show their devastating form.

Chernobyl disaster

The worst-ever nuclear disaster happened on 26th April, 1986, at exactly 01:23:45 am. Reactor number 4 exploded releasing tons of highly radioactive uranium into the atmosphere.

I have studied this disaster extensively during my graduation and frequently use it as an example to describe how important it is to know your job. I presented this disaster during graduation with the title 'Know Your Job.' Before I joined graduate school, I had almost two years of professional experience. So I knew how people do their jobs. The majority of people work without knowing much about their job till they have crossed the two or three-year mark. They do just what their supervisors ask them to do. This is what led the Chernobyl nuclear power plant to disaster and brought an entire continent to the edge of destruction.

Many reports point to two reasons for this accident, one is scientific and the other is human. The 5th episode of the Chernobyl documentary by HBO describes this in detail. Some aspects are given below.

- The plant director signed the commissioning completion papers without actual completion and allowed the reactor to commence its operation
- Despite three safety test failures, the reactor kept functioning
- The series of events that led to the disaster started when the electrical grid controller requested the postponement of the reduction. In other words, to hold a safety rundown test till midnight. The test was actually scheduled for the day shift but it was moved to the night shift at the last minute without assessing risks. They were working with radioactive materials and reactors that could destroy the entire continent and would threaten the world but they were nonchalant about the weight of their decisions
- This low-capacity run created a scientific reason for the disaster i.e. core poisoning (xenon accumulation in the core)
- There were human factors too. Imagine the situation when a 25-year-old engineer with hardly three months of experience is operating the reactor in the control room, that too for a safety test he wasn't aware of. Amazing! In contrast, you need a minimum of a year's relevant experience to get a forklift driving license in India since it's a safety matter
- The deputy chief engineer acted like a dictator. He violated all the safety practices and operational guidelines that were in place. This engineer was the hero of this disaster by violating all the managerial rules and forcing operators to override all the system signals
- Lastly, the design flaw in the reactor gave the final touch to the disaster

The last slide of my graduate presentation read, "There was no one in that control room on 26th April 1986 who knew what they were doing and how an RBMK reactor could explode!"

They seemed to be completely overconfident, overestimating the certainty. In the chapter on problem-solving, I walked you through both the certainty approach and uncertainty approach and asked you to focus on the former to make sure you know what you require clearly. But in the case of Chernobyl, they overestimated certainty and bypassed all the rules and standard practices. The system was completely and fatally flawed. The influencers didn't know about this flaw and went on to influence the system negatively. Was this an accident? No, it was an invitation to disaster!

Akash helped me prepare the presentation. We drew a Swiss cheese model to explain how defences were overridden to meet disaster. The Swiss cheese model is based on the principle of layered security. In many instances, one control is not enough to prevent risks, hence analyzing risks and their cause is necessary to improve system defences. The model is given below.

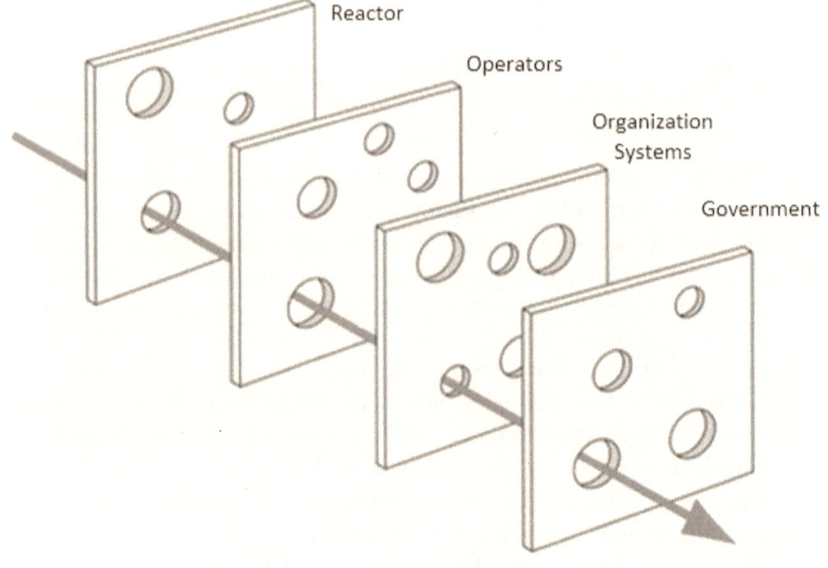

Figure 7.3

The Swiss cheese model is a great way to graphically represent the fact that no single safety defence is enough to prevent accidents. Every defence mechanism will have some degree of flaws, opportunities to override, and possibilities for ignoring signals. So, as system designers, it's our task to put in as many defences as possible so that overriding one or two doesn't lead to failure. I often use this model to draw a picture of systemic practices and their possible flaws. This is the picture we drew at the macro level in 2012. This was my very first exposure to this amazing tool. Today, I practice this at a highly micro level. I work with dozens of slices to study combinations, in different and potentially possible ways, to know how and when accidents or system failures happen. I am using this model for advanced risk assessment research, which is still under experimentation and testing, but once it is fully developed it will change the way we assess risks and improve system safety as well as influencers' safety.

The safer the influencers feel, the more confident they become and that makes them work more closely with the system and keep it working accurately and safely. Hence, ensuring the safety of the influencers is directly related to ensuring the system's safety. This is again systems psychology.

In Chernobyl, the reactor had a serious flaw and the operators or no one in the control room knew about it. They were completely unaware of how and when the reactor could explode. The organization system was reluctant to accept the fact that the reactor had exploded and no guidelines for when and how to take any important tests were available. At the broader level, the government protected all the lies that plant management was telling the world. The entire line of defence was full of holes.

Using the above-mentioned information if you draw the Swiss cheese model, you can understand that there are multiple ways that this accident could have happened as all four defence categories have several flaws, if not in one way the disaster would have taken place in some other way. Whenever you mark holes, ensure that the hole sizes and the numbers are in proportion to the degree of their probability of occurrence so that not just the position of the holes but their size also helps you capture potentially risky events.

I have just explained this for one case. You can go through the information I have provided here for each disaster and place it in the Swiss cheese model for your practice as well as for better understanding. Use this tool to improve your systems and organizational safety.

I am providing an extra chapter next to help you better understand the tools and concepts I have used throughout this book.

Chapter 8

Problem Solving – Part II

Swiss cheese model

This model has been used since the 1980s to analyze the causes of an incident and how it bypasses the defences of the system. In simple terms, it is a causation model. This model talks about two types of causes, active causes and latent or passive causes. Active causes directly trigger the incident whereas latent causes lie dormant in the system structure until they are triggered by some influences or support from the active causes, leading to incidents. Identification of the latent causes is very difficult. It requires complete expertise in the process and system and mastery over risk analysis tools like Failure Modes and Effects Analysis (FMEA), qualitative study of the system, and analytical skills in system analysis like cause and effect modelling, statistical modelling, etc. Active causes are easy but need extra care than usual just to ensure that we are not limiting our focus. Prior trouble data is a great way to broaden the coverage of causes.

We will get problems when flaws in the defences are aligned in a straight line from the first to the last slice. There are two ways to improve the system to prevent errors from happening. The first is to remove the flaws completely and develop an ideal system. We all know that this is very difficult to achieve. Ideal conditions are good for studies but practically it is a fact that it is next to impossible. If there are flaws, then stack multiple slices or defences, so that the flaws aren't aligned. The second way is the most practical way and this is what most system designers use i.e. to develop highly effective and high-efficiency systems.

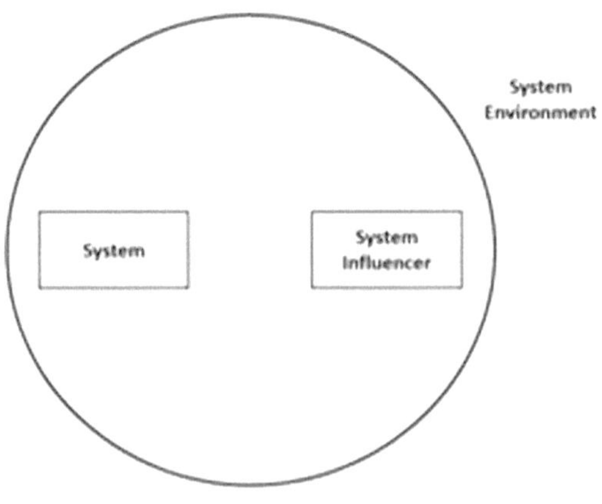

Figure 8.1

In the system diagram above, we have three factors to consider while we analyze any system—the system itself along with internal and external influencers. You have designed your organizational system with 6 basic considerations to achieve three fundamental characteristics (the fourth is for the advanced-level or learning systems). System designers cannot deny the fact that along with natural ones, there will also be forced influences. Natural influences are the flaws in system design when you haven't considered some factors and they allow for the production and passing of errors. Forced influences are those errors committed by influencers forcing the system like bypassing some controls or taking the system to such a situation where it generates errors. An excellent example of this is Chernobyl reactor number 4 where the operators and chief engineer led the reactor to disaster. How you can prevent the system from getting influenced by these types of influences? I will describe that here.

The forced influence in the Chernobyl disaster tells us a subtle story. Under conflicted influences, forced influence prevails as they come from indirect influencers and since they are higher authorities, you cannot ignore them. Even if you don't agree to do it, you may be compelled. These are called situational or circumstantial influences.

I am taking the same example I took earlier to describe the four-step problem-solving framework. Let me recall the full model here for better understanding. I will take you through each defence separately and discuss individual factors.

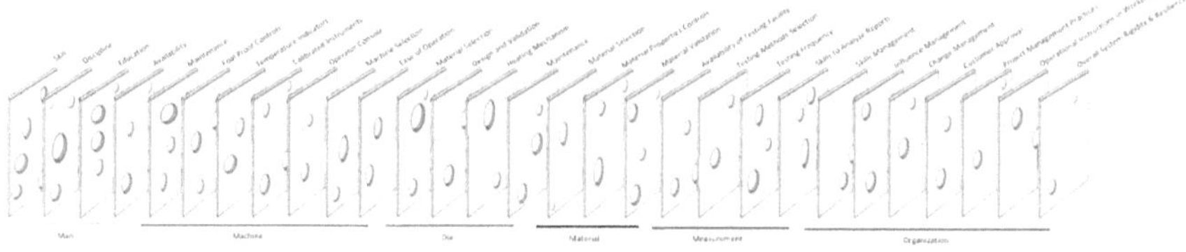

Figure 8.2

The above image is non-readable since I have considered multiple slices just to make sure that the model is better understood. It is better to see the system in its entirety and then begin its intrinsic systems analysis. Don't miss the view of the forest even if you are eager to study the individual trees.

I considered 6 categories of defences here

- Man
- Machine
- Die
- Material
- Measurement
- Organization (Organizational System)

Please note that I am taking only internal influencers here as the effect of external influencers is proportionally lesser than internal ones. If we strengthen internal influencers, most of the external influences also get covered. Also, in the example I have considered, the effect exerted by the environment is insignificant, so it is ignored. If needed, you can study it for your reference.

Let's look at each defence layer one by one.

Man or people

The flaws or opportunities for errors are very high in manpower. Every failure that I have analyzed and investigated till now has been linked to humans in one way or another. Humans are the main influencers in any system, whether organizational, manufacturing or intrinsic. Hence, I have marked more flaws in this category and as you can see, errors go through and if the next layer also has flaws, then it could lead to problems.

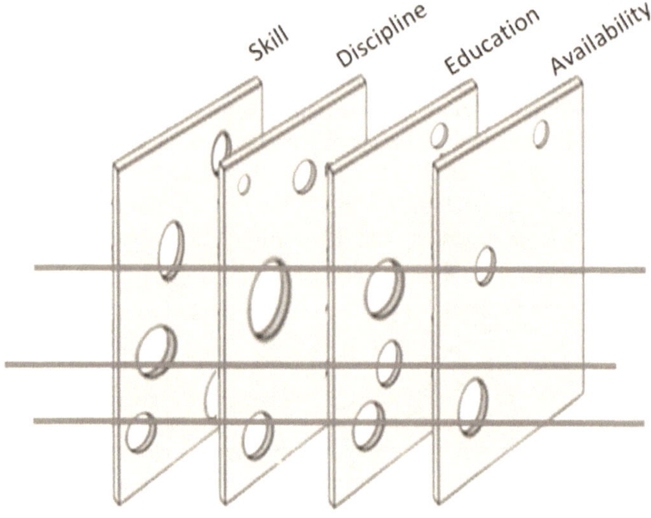

Figure 8.3

Here I have taken 4 defences: skill, discipline, education, and availability.

- **Skill:** The selection of a man, whether operator, helper, supervisor or any person whose work directly or indirectly influences or affects the product or the production system must have the appropriate skills necessary to do his/her job. Skill gaps are a very common reason across industries. Some indirect influencers like managers, top management, and other non-functional or supporting departments, depending on the situation, can also forcefully influence the system's defences by deviating from standard practices, as observed in the case of the Challenger space shuttle. If deviating from system practices becomes routine, it feeds a wrong message into the minds of the direct influencers and creates a new culture allowing further deviations. So whenever indirect influencers come into the picture they should not forcefully influence the practices. The skill gap across the supply chain contributed to this problem as well. Manufacturers didn't know what process they were running (systemically) and customers didn't know what they wanted.

- **Discipline:** This word has multiple meanings, but as of now, we will consider the meaning as 'sincerity to follow what is mentioned in the standard system practices.' People become undisciplined due to various reasons. Two of the important ones are repeated force influences that feed in the wrong message, and stubbornness (whatever you say he does what he wants to do). The cases of indiscipline that I have found till now were initiated by a higher level of influencers like supervisors, managers, or even top management. They specifically bypass some practices and then blame the operators. Discipline is too broad in its scope and must be known to all. One must have the sincerity to follow systemic practices and this applies to everyone under the organizational roof, from the CEO to the operator.
- **Education:** Every person who works directly on the system must know what he is doing, and for that he needs education. Normally what happens is that the people who work and influence directly are illiterates or don't know their job adequately and indirect influencers have two degrees! My question is, who is influencing your system directly? Since managers are indirect influencers, their education only matters when people below them know their job, otherwise what they do is a last-minute system bypass. In one of my investigations, I found that the customers had lowered their requirements when the suppliers were unable to fulfil them. A few months later their product failed and the lowered requirement was the cause of the failure. In my investigation report, I mentioned, "Please stop a dangerous culture of 'if all else fails, lower your goals'."
- **Availability:** Adequate manpower must be available to reduce human fatigue. Psychological experiments clearly show that once fatigued, the ability of the physical body as well as the creativity of the mind drops significantly. Both allowing overtime and running with low numbers matter equally.

This list is not exhaustive but I have put across these four just for the sake of conceptual understanding. The more the number of defences, the lesser the opportunity for errors to pass through. For better prevention of errors, increase defences but ensure fewer negative influences as despite more defences a proportionately greater number of forceful influences will not protect the system. One of the main reasons for bypassing the standard practices is unnecessary restrictions, as that creates system traffic and people choose to bypass or negatively influence the system. Do not overstretch any system. The third C in my 3C concept says no constraints, which means no unnecessary constraints.

Machine

In many product-centred systems, machine defence is very important to analyze any problems, but in this case, the machine is an intrinsic system. I have taken seven layers of defence—maintenance, fool/error proof controls, temperature indicators, calibrated instruments, operator console, machine selection, and ease of operation.

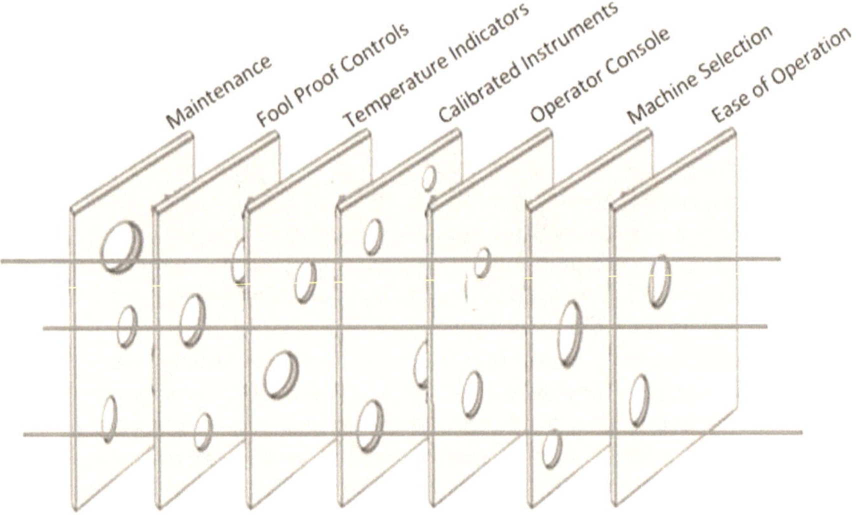

Figure 8.4

- **Maintenance:** The health of the machine is ensured by maintenance. Whatever method you follow has to have some basic considerations, like, a preformatted list of checkpoints, defined frequency, the skill of the staff, guidelines to follow, etc. Some years ago, I visited an Indian Air Force workshop where I found a beautiful line, "Poor Maintenance is Murder." Whether you are maintaining an aircraft or a lathe machine this applies equally. A poorly maintained lathe machine is as deadly as a poorly maintained aircraft.
- **Fool/error-proof controls:** This defence has been focussed on in recent days as quality expectations are increasing. We don't want any error to damage our company's reputation. Despite having error-proofing controls, the system can produce mistakes if the maintenance is not up to the mark. In some random situations, even the best error-proofing controls can allow errors. Hence, having a parallel systemic defence is also necessary. This is an important advantage of using the Swiss cheese model. You can check different combinations by deleting some defences and see what happens. Lacking any necessary systemic defence means the failure of the complete system.
- **Temperature indicators:** Indicators give you a direct measurement that you would have otherwise taken through thermometers or portable pyrometers. In the extrusion bracket failure, the role of the temperature indicator was vital as there was no measurement provision for exit metal at all (during my first process visit). They installed it later but the measurements were contradictory. A defence that is available but corrupted cannot protect the system.
- **Calibrated instruments:** I already mentioned how to make correct decisions and my preferred method is through accessibility, reliability, and usability. Whenever you take any measurements to ensure their reliability, check whether the instruments were calibrated or not. Erroneous reference can only intensify

the negative influence. Remember, wrong numbers used in the right way kill faster than the right numbers used in the wrong way.

- **Operator console**: Machines need electronic operator consoles so that the operator can see what's going on in the machine and can control things. Some machines come with multiple consoles that make tasks difficult, so ensure consolidation of consoles.
- **Machine selection:** The right machine selection is an important task for quality products.
- **Ease of operation:** I have seen some machines with Chinese letters and numbers, which makes operation difficult and limits the operational understanding to only a few people.

In this category, as you can see in the image above, more defences prevent the error from passing through. You can remove some defences and see if the error could pass easily. This list is not exhaustive though. You can add if required as per your process and machine but ensure that you have enough defence layers in place to prevent the holes or flaws from aligning, preventing errors.

Die—this is a product-centred system in this problem

In chapter 4, you saw that I considered the die as a system, a thermodynamic system, for my analysis. Whenever you analyze any problem, check whether the problem is related to the product or product usage/application. You can do this through preliminary tests or, in most cases, through close observation. You can tell what's the issue and where to focus, but make sure you don't jump directly to a conclusion or write your problem statement. Failed parts or any symptoms are just an indication that something is wrong somewhere. The broken part is not the problem, it's the victim. The culprit is hidden somewhere else. It's the investigators who need to find the culprit and provide justice for the damaged part.

In this category of defence, I have listed four types of defence—material selection, design and validation, heating mechanism, and maintenance.

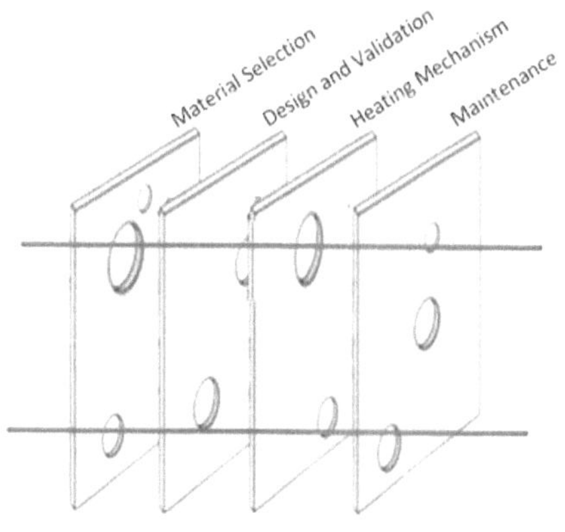

Figure 8.5

I will discuss only the design factor here as the other three do not contribute as much.

Design and Validation: After my investigation and tests, I concluded that the die design was the problem. Unknowingly they had designed a high-pressure die with a low fusion gap. The lesson for me, my client, and the extruder was pretty much clear. Even after having over 6 decades of experience in the industry, they didn't know that they were designing a system. This was the real problem that led to that failure. Whenever we design any tools, we should analyze them and consider them in terms of a system. We should consider the technical concepts of that system and validate the results, not just 'Ok' and 'not-ok,' but listen to what those numbers are whispering. Every failure says something. As systems thinkers, you should have eyes that see and ears that listen. This is why I am giving you this **third eye**. With just calm and clear observation, you can find clues that directly take you to the problem or at least to the concerns. I will share the tools that I use to support my observational ability. I use the cut-up technique to avoid disorientations, control charts or trend charts to see where the next points will be and the Swiss cheese model to analyze whether the available defences are adequate or not and look for possible combinations that can let errors through. I also take advantage of the cognitive vibration that I described in the previous chapters and many others. All of these techniques don't demand high experience or advanced education. Just hold the things in your hand and try to speak to them. Even a stone could tell you its story if you want to listen to it.

Material

Material is one of the basic considerations that need to be taken care of in early product and process validation. Once you validate, get it documented and review available defences to ensure the integrity of the system. In my investigation, the material wasn't the problem but the one-letter difference took me to the problem. There was a material change but that was because of the die design. Initially, they were running with good material (high strength) but when they start facing issues they changed it. Observation again played a role here. I have personally experienced that what you can see through your eyes cannot be detected even by an advanced machine. This is because of various reasons, one of which is generative intelligence.

In this category of defence, I have listed three defences—material selection, material properties controls, material validation

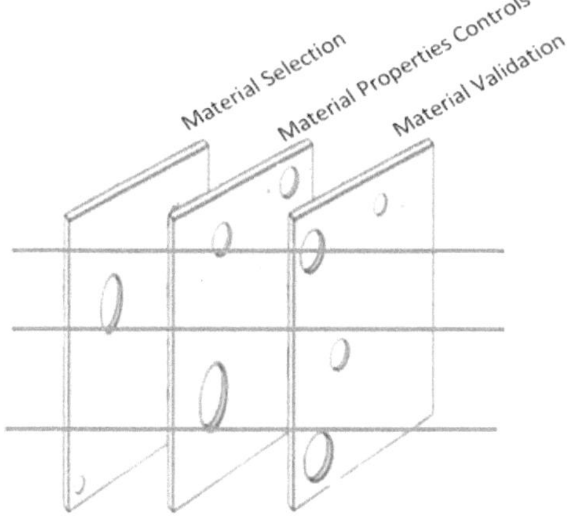

Figure 8.6

I am emphasizing material selection here as this is another major contributing factor apart from die design in this failure. The die designers referred to the wrong material specifications while designing it, because of a lack of systemic understanding. The designers were unaware that they are designing a system. Even if we ignore this error, they should have analyzed the reason 'why' they were getting die pressure issues and the system stalled but unfortunately, they ignored that too. Instead of going for analysis, they jumped the rope and changed the material directly.

Measurement

In this category of defence, I have listed four slices. I have not provided the individual explanations here as availability and skills have been covered under the 'man' category whereas method selection and testing frequency are related to the organization-centred system.

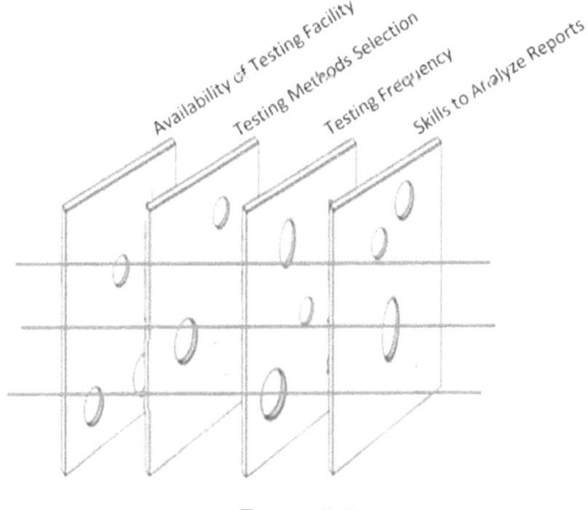

Figure 8.7

Organization (Organizational System)

So far, we have seen five categories of defences that are related to the product-centred system and its intrinsic systems. Now we are going to discuss an organization-centred system. These two systems are largely interrelated and one directly affects the other. Though it looks like you are selling products, in reality, if you see through the systemic approach or the **third eye**, you can see that your customers are buying your system, and you are selling them your system. The quality of your system is the quality of your product on which your customers place their confidence. Customers are buying systems, in other words, they are buying confidence by paying you money! Don't ever make them lose that confidence.

In this category of defence, I have listed seven layers—skills management, influence management, change management, customer approval, project management practices, operational instructions in workplaces, and overall system rigidity and resilience.

You can say that the defences listed here have been covered in one or another way in individual categories. That is why these are interrelated systems. In your organizational system, you have a bird's eye view or you zoom out, whereas in intrinsic systems or product-centred systems, you zoom in to see that particular product or that particular intrinsic system. Looking at the entire Great Banyan Tree is like looking through the organizational system and looking at individual prop roots is similar to an intrinsic system's view. The confidence of the intrinsic system is the strength of your organizational system and in turn that organizational system strength supports all those intrinsic systems.

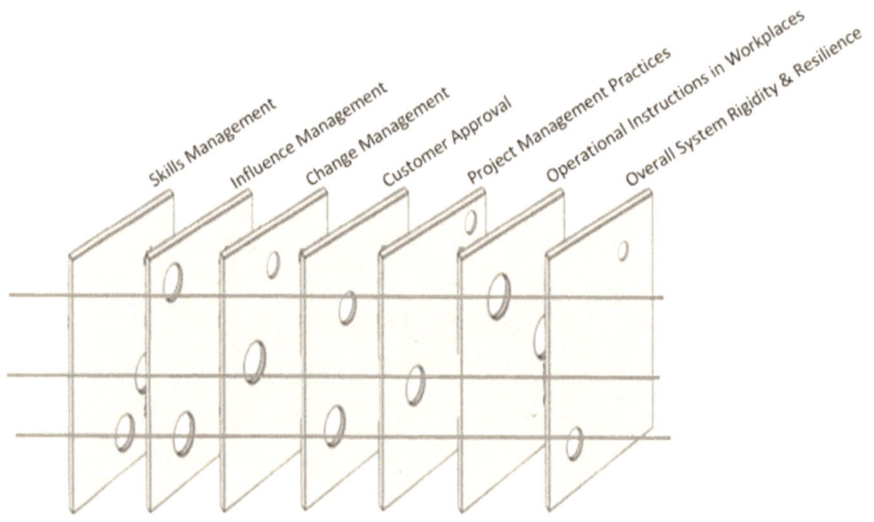

Figure 8.8

Organization-wide systems talk mainly about how all those individual intrinsic systems are managed. Some may say it is mainly documentation or paperwork but it is beyond that. Though it is necessary, in our day-to-day work we may not be serious about our individual intrinsic system's defences. Some may not function as desired and some may completely be removed. There are many other possibilities. When it comes to the organizational system, we verify these through various audits and ensure that they are in place and are aligned with requirements and functioning well.

You might have remembered how our standard weight is preserved. The master level standard, International Prototype of the Kilogram (IPK), is protected by the International Bureau of Weights and Measures (BIPM), Paris. It is only used to calibrate national standards once in 40 years. These national standards are used for the calibration of secondary standards and so on. Those master and primary standards never come out and are never used for general-purpose measurements. The organizational systems also do the same. They are used to calibrate the working systems or intrinsic systems and once everything is okay, it acts as an additional defence. The organizational system I refer to here does not mean the certifications you have, but rather the practices you follow. After all, your certifications cannot defend your system, your practices can. So, don't be proud of displaying certificates in galleries and on websites, keep this in mind and allow your customers to be confident.

Along with risk analysis, I use this model in system analysis and improvements. In this case, the die has a design flaw because of which they had changed the metal chemistry but did not record and validate this change. Both these flaws coincided, but if the operating instructions were clear enough to check the exit temperature of the extrusion, and if they had known that thermodynamic equilibrium equation, then the problem would have been prevented. Consider that it wasn't followed. Let's see how the next defence would have been used. Up to some extent the metal also defends itself before it exhibits the defect. Even if the defect is not starkly visible, its strength would be lesser as the metal is experiencing transformation resulting in coarse grains. If they would have followed standard test practices and compared material strength to that of the standard, they would have known that there was a problem. This defence layer was also breached. Every system gives signals, and a system breakdown or failure is rarely unannounced.

After modelling the system, all I did was draw a rough diagram of the Swiss cheese model and check the various defence combinations. I found better defences with some combinations and in the second trial tested and validated my hypotheses about which layer was affecting the system in which ways. Even with the same die, after studying and modelling the system and the Swiss cheese model, I ensured it produced the highest quality material.

Thus the Swiss cheese model helps you analyze your defences and identifies how the flaws could lead to failure. As I said in the introduction, until now this model was used for accident investigations and risk analysis, but now I am bringing it to operational failure analysis through a systemic approach. I think it can become a great tool if understood in depth and made a part of the failure investigation. In this book, I have given many unique approaches to study, understand, and use systemic approaches to work as well as to solve problems.

We prepare FMEAs, a tool used to assess potential failure modes, effects, and controls. But we just stop there, we don't go further to study how the combinations of failure modes could create new situations and influence the system. This is what I wanted to convey through factor categorization. Each category of factors occurs for different reasons and influences the system in specific ways. When two or more factors combine, they can influence the system in different ways. On the other hand, shadow factors and latent factors influence the system in some other ways. This type of factor categorization and system analysis takes us to the very depth and breadth of our process, quality, and system in its entirety. It is really very difficult to grasp the depth of this analysis. You might think that this combination analysis will stretch to an endless game, but that is not so. In fact, it is even shorter than your detailed FMEA! It's just a matter of understanding and the way you assess the risks. Don't use dozens of tools and techniques, but use those few that will give maximum effectiveness.

Every non-systemic solution of ours incurs a debt to the systems and the system knows how to get it back.

Keep building and strengthening your organizational systems. And, more importantly, keep learning…

If I ever learned any lesson from solving problems, it would be that you can never solve any problem by running away. You can only solve them by running towards them.

Nothing is more important to me than changing the way we solve problems and spreading and influencing learning everywhere. The definition of life in my terms is Learn, Work, and Teach. It's the **third eye** from Shivalingeshwar.

Success comes not from being the best, nor does it come from being lucky. You need to put in your best effort and keep everything else aside. This lesson from the Gita says it all.

कर्मण्येवाधिकारस्ते मा फलेषु कदाचन
मा कर्मफलहेतुर्भूर्मा ते सङ्गोऽस्त्वकर्मणि

karmaṇy evādhikāras te
mā phaleṣu kadācana
mā karma-phala-hetur bhūr
mā te saṅgo 'stv akarmaṇi

Acknowledgement

Just like any other book based on research, I too have many people to thank. Writing The Third Eye was one thing and writing this note of thanks was another as I had to recall every memory. Some made me feel proud and some brought tears.

The question I had when I started writing this note of thanks was, "Whom should I thank first?" In other words, "Who gave me The Third Eye?"

After scouring through thousands of memories, I prepared a short list of names. The first person I should thank is the one who gave me the courage to dream and hones my perception beyond the ordinary. This was none other than the late Kudabale sir from my primary school. He was my class teacher from the third to the seventh standard. His unique style of teaching by connecting with his students was exceptional. One instance made a lasting impact on my life. Somewhere in fifth or sixth grade, I did something that angered him. So he called me into his chamber. I thought he'd punish me but instead, he asked, "What are your dreams? Who do you want to become?"

I didn't have answers to those questions then.

Even today, whenever I pass by that crumbling school building, I remember Kudabale sir's questions. His two unanswered questions set me on a mission to find my dreams and find 'who I want to become.' This is what a real teacher can do to you.

If Kudabale sir had been with us today, I could have taken the first copy of this book to him and answered the questions he had asked nearly two decades ago. Thank you, sir.

Along with him, many other teachers from my school and college contributed to my educational foundation. From Chalavadi sir who taught me how to sit in the classroom when I was in the second standard to Dr. S. Mohankumar, the principal of SDMCET Dharwad at that time, who signed my project proposal when I approached him. He gave his approval while bypassing the HOD Heblikar sir. The latter had not approved my project since it was related to electronics and I was from mechanical engineering. Everyone played their role perfectly which ultimately made me reach this level. I should have dedicated this book to all my teachers but instead of listing all the names I just wrote one name, my Master, Srila Prabhupada. Somewhere I read that the spiritual master comes to you in various forms to make sure you are set on the right path and for the time being he appeared in his original form to give me higher direction. Thanks to all my teachers.

I met my first systems thinking mentor, Akash Singh, in 2011. His best lesson was, "Never fear problems. If you have heard that there's something wrong then become the first one to jump in and solve it." He used to remind me often, "Shiva, if you don't want to see problems, it doesn't mean you should close your eyes, but solve them."

I met him last time in February 2012. While sitting in my room in Dharwad just a few days before that last meeting, he told me, "Good teachers are those who get great students." But I argued, "Good students are those who have great teachers." It's a kind of transcendental relationship, one praises the other.

Thank you, Akash.

I must thank all the companies I worked with, especially Sujan CoperStandard AVS, Pune and Innova Rubbers, Nashik. I learned and practised most of the concepts in The Third Eye during those years. My bosses in both these companies never placed tight controls over me. They knew that I loved solving problems and, except for very few occasions, they allowed me to fly. That was the kind of freedom I had and that made all the difference. Some of my findings may hurt them but please bear with me as I uncovered these things for only one purpose—to solve problems. I always believe, "When it comes to solving problems, it's not about who is right and who is wrong. What matters is whether the problems are solved or not." I always worked to save the company or the system, not my seat.

I must also thank all the suppliers that I worked with in my 7-year career. Their innovative ways of generating problems allowed me to develop innovative solutions. I always followed my approach and believed, "Instead of blaming others find your way to deal with problems and you'll learn." One professor in Nashik told me, "If everything is well and good, there's no need for intelligent people. You are here because there are problems. So, instead of blaming others and complaining, use the opportunities to learn."

'The heart is the stupidest thing.' During my busy schedule, I also fell in love, but by the time I understood that I was in love, it was too late to reconcile. It took me months to come out of that shock. My Master, Srila Prabhupada gave a defined direction to my life in those difficult days so steer me away from the wrong path. Holding The Third Eye in my hand, if I look back at those days, I feel I'm lucky to let it go. I believe, "Great things come to you at the cost of good things." In my life, that love was just like an astronomical object that came on my path to deliver a slingshot effect. Thank you, baby.

I don't believe in fate. "What you choose during your difficult times decides where you will end up." I chose my Master and he changed everything. Just one ray from a spiritual master's divine grace can change anything and everything.

I thank my parents, sister (Kavita), and brother (Chetan) for their unwavering support. I'm so fortunate to have you who backed me always.

And, last but not least, I thank all the staff of Notion Press Publications. Ms Charmine Joseph (my marketing contact), Mr Waseem (my publication manager), Ms Anupama Rajesh, my editor, and all the backend staff who worked to make this book a reality. I would pass a special thanks to Ms Anupama Rajesh for her patience in understanding and editing my words. Thank you, team. The Third Eye journey has just begun. I hope I will work with you on upcoming editions.

Everyone that I interviewed as part of my research told me that two phases of life are the most memorable—one's childhood and life as a student.

Henry Ford said, "Anyone who stops learning is old, whether at twenty or eighty. Anyone who keeps learning stays young. The greatest thing in life is to keep your mind young."

Thanks to all the readers of The Third Eye.

Through The Third Eye, I welcome you all once again to these two beautiful phases of our lives. Be a child and be a student. And, never let the learning stop. Please! Always keep reading.

I would like to make an additional note, especially for my critics. I have written this book as an introduction or say, a concise edition. I have given very limited references. But, as far as possible, I have tried to conceptualize lessons using generalized scientific concepts and theories and used general examples to bring clarity. In some places wherever absolutely necessary I have given references as well. I assure you, nothing in this book is without a sufficient scientific basis.

Author Bio

Shivalingeshwar Naik, an engineer by profession, turned to psychology later. He has over 7 years of professional experience in Supplier Management and Project Management roles. However, his interest in solving problems and improving suppliers through a systemic approach drove him towards studying systems from a psychological perspective. He states, "When it comes to improvement, quality is a psychology." He was also an entrepreneur and had initiated 3 short-lived enterprises. He, however, left the business side of things at a very early stage in order to continue with his research.

Taking the advice of his mentor seriously, he found a peculiar way of researching systems. Instead of going through a university, he delved into workplaces where he could see and study actual systems. Since he was from a supplier management background, this approach was easy and turned out to be an opportunity for his research. This peculiar way of studying systems helped him analyze systems structure more deeply. Since organizations don't study systems as they should, he is working on generalizing his findings and systems lessons through his projects on organizational learning and systems psychology by using scientific concepts. The Third Eye is his first publication which aims to introduce his research.

www.ingramcontent.com/pod-product-compliance
Lightning Source LLC
LaVergne TN
LVHW091325150826
845673LV00006B/1772